"What couple hasn't struggled from time to time with praying together? *When Couples Pray* is a must-read for any husband and wife who desire a closer relationship with each other. Read, let it sink into your heart, and experience a oneness with your mate and God like you've never experienced before!"

DR. GARY AND BARBARA ROSBERG
HOSTS OF *AMERICA'S FAMILY COACHES...LIVE!* AND
COAUTHORS, *THE 5 LOVE NEEDS OF MEN AND WOMEN*

"It's always nice to know we're not alone in our marriage struggles, that someone understands, and that answers can be found. Cheri Fuller's easy-to-read book comes alongside in just this way. Readers can identify with and apply godly truths to solving similar challenges as they strengthen their Christian homes."

LYNDA HUNTER BJORKLUND
AUTHOR, SPEAKER, SYNDICATED COLUMNIST

"*When Couples Pray* is not another guilt-charged book chiding couples on the need to pray together. Loaded with encouragement, *When Couples Pray* shows in a 'come-alongside way' both the struggles and results of couples who began praying together. Speaking as a typical man who is not naturally driven to intimacy, *When Couples Pray* made me want to initiate this practice in my own marriage. I heartily recommend this book to you; it will make a difference in your marriage."

JONATHAN GRAF
EDITOR, *PRAY!* MAGAZINE

D1530857

Also by Cheri Fuller

WHEN COUPLES PRAY

The Little-Known Secret
to Lifelong
Happiness in Marriage

Multnomah®Publishers *Sisters, Oregon*

CHERI FULLER

WHEN COUPLES PRAY

published by Multnomah Publishers, Inc.
in association with the literary agency of Alive Communications, Inc.
7680 Goddard Street, Suite 200, Colorado Springs, CO 80920

© 2001 by Cheri Fuller
International Standard Book Number: 1-57673-666-0

Cover image by Christine Alicino/Photonica

Scripture quotations are from:
The Holy Bible, New International Version © 1973, 1984 by International Bible Society,
used by permission of Zondervan Publishing House

Also quoted:
The Holy Bible, New King James Version (NKJV) © 1984 by Thomas Nelson, Inc.
The Living Bible (TLB) © 1971. Used by permission of Tyndale House Publishers, Inc.
All rights reserved.
The Message © 1993 by Eugene H. Peterson
The New Testament in Modern English, Revised Edition (Phillips)
© 1958, 1960, 1972 by J. B. Phillips.
The Amplified Bible (AMP) © 1965, 1987 by Zondervan Publishing House.
Holy Bible, New Living Translation (NLT) © 1996. Used by permission of
Tyndale House Publishers, Inc. All rights reserved.
New American Standard Bible (NASB) © 1960, 1977 by The Lockman Foundation

Multnomah is a trademark of Multnomah Publishers, Inc.
and is registered in the U.S. Patent and Trademark Office.
The colophon is a trademark of Multnomah Publishers, Inc.

For information:
MULTNOMAH PUBLISHERS, INC.•POST OFFICE BOX 1720•SISTERS, OREGON 97759

Library of Congress Cataloging-in-Publication Data
Fuller, Cheri. When couples pray : the little known secret to lifelong
happiness in marriage / by Cheri Fuller. p.cm.
Includes bibliographical references.   ISBN 1-57673-666-0 (pbk.)
1. Spouses—Religious life. 2. Prayer—Christianity. 3. Marriage—Religious
aspects—Christianity. I. Title. BV4596.M3 F85 2001 248.8'44—dc21 00-011255

02 03 04 05 06 — 10 9 8 7 6 5 4 3 2 1

To Holmes

prayer partner, faithful husband, marvelous father, best friend.

Acknowledgments

A book is not written in a vacuum. It's a team effort, and I want to thank the team who helped make this book a reality. Jeff Leeland planted the seed; Dee Brestin watered it and encouraged me greatly. Dan Benson and Nancy Thompson, my terrific editors, Bill Jensen, and the Multnomah team brought the project into full bloom. Thank you! My heartfelt thanks also to Greg Johnson, my agent, for his support and encouragement and to all those couples who shared their stories of what happened when they prayed. My thanks wouldn't be complete without including my husband, Holmes, for being my companion on this spiritual journey and for being so willing all those times I said, "Honey, let's pray."

CONTENTS

INTRODUCTION

How to Get the Most from This Book

Last weekend, we attended yet another wedding. In a gorgeous silk and brocade dress, the glowing bride floated down the aisle to the sound of trumpets and organ music to meet her groom at the altar. Candles flickered as the couple gazed into each other's eyes and promised to love forever.

Just as it is at every wedding, my heart was touched by the commitment and love of the bride and groom. I have to confess that as the wedding songs were sung, the vows spoken, the four-tiered wedding cake consumed, and the rosebuds showered upon the couple as they raced away in a rented limo, the thought *Do they really know what they're getting into?* crossed my mind. Actually, most of us *don't* really know what we're getting into, or we might not say, "I do"! Although marriage can be fulfilling, it is also hard work—sometimes much harder than we had anticipated.

When two people decide to become "one," they actually become a new entity. Their oneness is something that can deeply satisfy both husband and wife as well as serve God's purposes. Yet because they are imperfect people in a fallen world, this new entity faces incredible challenges from within and without. The couple must deal with each other's weaknesses and differences. Their sin natures war against their unity. Selfishness, childhood wounds, or bitterness may oppose their best efforts to become one.

From without, a couple may be assailed by situations that can strain any marriage—serious, chronic illness, the loss of a child, business calamities, overloaded schedules, and career pressures. They also are surrounded by a society that calls marriage irrelevant and says, "If it doesn't work out or make you happy, it's okay to call it quits." The cultural pressures to cheat, get divorced, or go after material things instead of spiritual values can lead many couples to part ways in spite of their best intentions.

There are also spiritual attacks against this oneness. The enemy comes to kill, steal, and destroy—and not just in our individual lives, but in our marriages and families as well. To counter his attack, we need the spiritual ammunition of prayer. "For though we walk (live) in the flesh, we are not carrying on our warfare…using mere human weapons. For the weapons of our warfare are not physical…but they are mighty before God for the overthrow and destruction of strongholds" (2 Corinthians 10:3–4, AMP).

The reality is that half of all marriages today *do* end in divorce, both for Christians and non-Christians. Studies show that simply attending church does not guarantee a happy marriage or divorce-proof a relationship. However, couples who pray together regularly report enjoying the most satisfying marriages of all—and the divorce rate for praying couples is less than 1 percent![1]

All of us face obstacles and challenges in our marriages. But the good news is that *God is for you.* He wants your marriage to succeed, to be fulfilling, and to reflect His glory to the world around you. And He offers incredible resources of grace, power, and boundless amounts of forgiveness so that you can truly live in peace and harmony instead of in anger and bitterness. He has an inexhaustible storehouse of love, wisdom, and provision for every single day of your life—even new mercies every morning!

The key to accessing all these resources for your marriage and family is *prayer*. Prayer is the way you keep the unity candle lit, so to speak. It is the way you invite God into your everyday life and continue the dialogue with Him and your mate that began in that wonderful season of "first love" that brought you to the altar.

It's like the huge generator one of the kids in our prayer class drew to show what he had learned about prayer. "That's God," Grant said. "He's got all this power for us." Then he drew a long diagonal line from the huge generator to a few stick figures representing a family. "That's who needs help. And the power flows along the cord as we pray."

Out of the mouths of babes! That's exactly how it works. Prayer will bring God's power to your house! Whatever your age or stage of life, praying together as a couple is a powerful, little-known secret to lifelong happiness in marriage. It will help keep your marriage alive and well—even rekindle your love if the flame has died. Praying as a couple is a doorway to intimacy.

Through prayer we can still receive God's highest blessings and purposes in our marriage. Through prayer we keep the candles lit, nurturing our love relationship.

DAVID AND HEATHER KOPP

Of course, there are many other ways to build a strong marriage: spending time together, meeting your spouse's needs, writing love notes to each other, giving physical affection, keeping the romance alive. But prayer is the glue that binds everything together. It is the catalyst for God's power and blessing to be released in your life.

What are you thinking as you begin to read this book? Perhaps you don't feel successful at praying as a couple. If so, let me assure you that you are normal and have lots of company. Maybe you are going in so many directions that you're not sure how to wedge in prayer. Again, join the crowd! Although most of us know that God wants us to pray as couples, the truth is that even people who have been Christians a long time struggle with it.

Wherever you are, if you've picked up this book for hope and encouragement and practical, bite-sized ideas for praying together, that's what you'll find. I won't spend the following pages expounding on all the reasons you *should* be praying together, nor will I attempt to make you feel guilty if you're not. Instead, I'm going to demonstrate—with true stories from my life with Holmes and the lives of other couples we've known—what happens when husbands and wives come together to pray. I think you'll catch the excitement as you read our stories.

In each of the thirty-one chapters, you'll find a true story, a Scripture, motivating quotes, and a prayer exercise designed to guide you in meaningful dialogue with your spouse and God. You may want to read the stories aloud to each other for a devotional time. Or you might prefer to share them over coffee in the morning, before you turn out the lights at bedtime, or as you travel together. Then try the prayer exercise that accompanies each story and expect God to work in your life.

A husband and wife can experience true oneness only as they live by faith, in the power of the Holy Spirit.

DENNIS RAINEY

I've also sprinkled some prayers throughout the book. Read them for inspiration, or make them your own as you seek the Lord in prayer together.

Some of the stories will give you ideas about how you can pray regularly for your spouse in the midst of a busy, hectic schedule. Others will help you address prayer problems that couples typically experience—like feeling awkward about praying aloud or the challenge of having different prayer styles. Whether you're talkative or not, experienced at prayer or a brand-new believer, this book will refresh your spiritual life together—or jumpstart it, if that's what it needs.

What if you bought this book, but your spouse is reluctant to pray—more interested in her latest craft project or his TV ball game than prayer time? Instead of approaching your spouse with an attitude that conveys, "You don't pray with me enough, you spiritual sluggard, so I'm going to take charge of this," remember that it's the gentle, loving, quiet spirit that wins a partner over. "I want to share" messages are usually more effective than scolding, nagging, or giving orders. For example:

- "Here, dear. This story meant a lot to me [or was so inspiring to me]...I want to share it with you" could open the door to reading one of the devotionals together.
- "Honey, I need to pray with you about something that's worrying me." Or maybe a note left on the pillow saying, "By the way, I'd really like us to pray together for the kids once a week. Let's go out for breakfast Saturday morning and try it then." Most men or women, once they understand their husband or wife's need, will respond favorably.

If you are married to someone who, despite your best efforts, avoids praying with you or is disinterested in spiritual matters, let me encourage you to keep praying for your spouse. Know that when you're feeling alone in the prayer closet, heaven is watching, and the God of the universe is listening. *You are not alone!* In fact, the spiritual reality is that when you pray—with or without your spouse—you are joining Jesus in intercession. He's seated at the right hand of the Father making intercession for you (Hebrews 7:25), and He makes a terrific prayer partner!

Our divine Prayer Partner does not want us to give up praying for that reluctant spouse. He urges us to be like the persistent widow who, in her determination to receive justice from the unrighteous judge, kept on knocking, seeking, and asking. And Christ assures us that the One who sees what we do in secret will reward us openly (Matthew 6:6) if we *P-U-S-H: Pray Until Something Happens!*

As you read the chapters that follow, I'm confident that you will discover—as Holmes and I did—that with your first halting attempts and baby steps, God goes to work. As you invite Him into your life and marriage through prayer, He will prove incredibly faithful. He'll work in your jobs, your children's lives, your finances, and your difficult situations. But first and foremost, God will work *in you*.

The form your couple prayer takes is not important. That's why we've shown you a number of different ways. What matters is that you find a way that helps you open yourself to the huge storehouse of Grace that God has for you when you pray.

So as you read the stories, be aware that it's not just the blessing of *answered prayer* that's important. Watch also for what *prayer itself* does inside the soul of your marriage, building and bonding your relationship as God brings His life and presence into it. One of the most vital things prayer does is change our hearts and draw us to the Lord. And as each of us moves toward God in prayer, we grow closer to each other, and the unity candle remains lit. God's blessing will touch your family for generations to come, and His eternal purposes will be fulfilled.

That's what happens when couples pray.

In the Beginning

Can two walk together, unless they are agreed?

AMOS 3:3, NKJV

I paced around our little kitchen, fussed with the fresh flowers in the centerpiece I had placed on the table, and checked the chicken divan—*again*. Holmes and I had been married on Thanksgiving weekend, and now, a week after our wedding, we were back at home in Waco. Even though I had taught junior high students all day, I was determined that Holmes would come home from his job to a home-cooked meal.

Holmes always gets off at six o'clock, I thought. *Surely he'll be here in a few minutes. It's only a five-minute drive from the store. He's gonna love this casserole!*

7:00 P.M. *Where is he?* When I was growing up, being on time for dinner was expected. At our house, not showing up constituted a crime approaching mutiny. *Surely he'll be home soon.*

8:00 P.M. Still no Holmes. And no phone call. *I hope nothing's happened. I'd better call the store. No answer. I'll just rewarm the casserole when he gets here.*

9:00 P.M. I sat alone at the dining table, my spirits as limp as the green salad.

Slowly, the hours passed. My first-ever chicken divan, once creamy and hot, was now rubbery and cold. I had already reheated it several times while I waited for Holmes to come home.

At ten o'clock Holmes finally arrived, looking a little sheepish. He explained somewhat glibly that he had stopped off at the Lake Air Grill with the guys from the store. After one look at the food, he announced that he wasn't hungry—he had already had a burger. I had been worried that he had been in a car wreck; now I was hurt, angry, and in tears.

But when I tried to tell Holmes how I felt, he retreated into his shell like a turtle. I couldn't believe it—we had communicated so well before the wedding! Obviously not willing to discuss it, Holmes turned on the TV. When I became even more upset, he walked into the bedroom, closed the door, and went to bed. So much for the honeymoon! My tears turned to sobs.

With minor variations, this scene repeated itself throughout our first years of marriage. Gradually, brick by brick, the walls grew between us. Oh, there were many happy moments too—the births of our two sons, outings to the park, pushing the kids in their strollers around the neighborhood, and an occasional weekend trip to my parents' ranch in east Texas. I remember how thrilled I felt when Holmes returned home after several months of basic training and a two-week summer camp with the Airborne National Guard. But the closeness we had shared as an engaged couple had evaporated, and in times of stress or conflict, the distance between us seemed like a chasm too wide to bridge.

By our eighth anniversary, our marriage was in trouble. How I longed for conversation, intimacy, and a heart-to-heart connection with my husband! We shared the same bed, but I often felt as if we were a million miles apart.

I still remember the night when I realized that our marriage was at a crossroads. The lights were out, and Holmes was breathing softly next to me. I was full to the brim with bottled-up resentment, loneliness, and hurt. As I lay there thinking, I realized that I had a choice to make.

I could continue in the same direction I was going and pursue my own interests—postgraduate work, a women's writers' group, the tennis league. If I did, Holmes and I would probably become like "married singles"—living in the same house and functioning as parents but experiencing little closeness as a couple. Even worse, we might end up separated or divorced. Or, I could turn to God and seek *His* divine plan for our marriage. I had no idea then what God's divine plan might be, but I did recognize that it was an alternative.

The very next day I wiped the dust off a Phillips version of the New Testament and began to read it every afternoon while the boys took their naps. After I'd worked my way through the books of Matthew, Mark, and Luke—I read only a few chapters each day while the house was quiet—I began the book of John.

The biblical picture of marriage is the blending of two lives in the deepest possible way into a new unit that will both satisfy the individuals involved and serve the purposes of God in the highest possible manner.

GARY CHAPMAN

"At the beginning God expressed himself. That personal expression, that word, was with God and was God, and he existed with God from the beginning," I read silently. "All creation took place through him, and none took place without him. In him appeared life and this life was the light of mankind. The light still shines in the darkness and the darkness has never put it out" (John 1:1–5, Phillips).

As I continued reading the words of the first chapter, the eyes of my understanding were opened. In modern terms, the lights went on! (I realize now that this was no accident, because my faithful mom had been interceding for me for years.) The living Word, Jesus Himself, revealed Himself to me with a reality that left me breathless. I saw Him as the true Light who came into the world not only to bring light to *mankind's* darkness, but to bring it to *my* darkness.

Although I had been attending church, I had been living in a fog of skepticism and unbelief since my teenage years. Now, I suddenly knew that He was real. He was not a god who kept himself distant from us, nor was He merely a character of "biblical myth," as my religion professor had taught me. He was God's Son, He was with me, and He had a plan for my life. In those moments with my Savior, layers of doubt crumbled in His presence, and I yielded myself to Him anew.

With a hunger to know more of God, I dug into the Bible with more energy than I had ever expended in my favorite graduate courses in Shakespeare or Chaucer. Reading His Word daily renewed my thoughts. My perspective began to change. And apparently my husband must have noticed something was different, because without a word from me, he eagerly picked up the same New Testament and began to read it. A few weeks later, he found life in Jesus Christ.

For the miracle of prayer to begin operating in your life, one thing remains. You must pray.... Then, and only then, will your adventure in faith begin.

BILL HYBELS

And that was how the spiritual journey of our marriage started.

We didn't have a blueprint. We had no instruction. But God led us step-by-step. And one of the first places He led us was to our knees in prayer.

Although we had been churchgoers throughout our marriage, Holmes and I didn't know the first thing about praying together. We had uttered our own individual, silent "dart" prayers—as we raced to the emergency room with Justin during an asthma attack, or as we administered syrup of ipecac to our toddler, Chris, after he'd stuffed some dreadful-looking brown mushrooms into his little mouth. But we didn't have much experience talking calmly with God together, placing our needs and decisions before Him, listening for His answers, and gaining refreshment and renewal from unhurried time in His presence.

Holmes comes from a long line of people who were very private about their faith. By nature he was quiet; in a crisis or conflict, he said even less. As I discovered the night of the cold chicken divan, Holmes was a "move away" kind of person, while I was a "move toward" kind of person. I confronted; he retreated. When he moved away from me emotionally in stressful situations, I would feel scared and lonely. Then my emotions would run amok in verbal expression or in a torrent of worried thoughts that played over and over in my mind like a broken record.

We also had very different prayer styles. Holmes was more likely to "think" his prayers and be concise about it, whereas I could easily verbalize my petitions and be long-winded.

What a challenge it was for us to come together in prayer! Fortunately, what is impossible with man (and his wife) is possible with God!

Soon after our spiritual renewal began, Holmes received three job offers. One of them would mean another move. Even when I'm at my best, I hate moving; but at that particular time, I was nine months pregnant and carrying twenty-five extra pounds! At the end of a day corralling two preschool boys, I couldn't even *think* about packing boxes. And my nesting instincts were off the chart.

Move? No way! That was my position. A few months earlier we had moved to the house of my dreams, and all I wanted was to rock our soon-to-be-born baby on the porch of our red brick home with the white picket fence and watch the boys play in the bright autumn sunshine.

Holmes, however, knew that he was being squeezed out of his current job situation—the manager position that he had been promised wasn't materializing. With a growing family to support, he thought that we had to at least consider all of the new job offers. Besides that, he loved change—and enjoyed moving!

His usual method of decision making was to analyze everything internally, then announce what he'd figured out. I liked to hash everything out from all sides verbally and write lists of the pros and cons. Thankfully, our reconnection with God changed our way of dealing with these differences.

Perhaps for the first time in our marriage, Holmes came out on the porch, took my hand, and said, "Honey, let's pray together about these job offers. We need God's guidance. I just read today in James that if we need wisdom, we can ask God for it."

As we bowed our heads, a feeling of relief swept over me. We didn't have to make this decision on our own. We didn't have to be in conflict or watch helplessly as stress pushed us farther apart. There was someone who cared, someone who was bigger than us both, and I sensed that He was listening as we bowed our heads.

Holmes and I were just babies in prayer at that point. We were not experienced at talking to God and certainly not eloquent. But as we prayed our simple prayers, asking God to guide us, He not only was faithful to help us agree on which job Holmes should take, but He also did even more than we had asked.

The job Holmes accepted did mean that we would have to move. So we did—when baby Alison was only three weeks old. But grace smoothed the way. In fact, Holmes's new employer offered to help us find a house, and he personally arranged for a loan. Before the move we had been renting, with little hope of accumulating a large enough down payment to purchase our own home. With the new employer's help, we were able to buy the new house. We landed in a friendly neighborhood with other young families, not far from a church where our newfound faith could grow.

But God's direct answer to our prayer, wonderful as it was, was not the most important result of our praying together. Even more precious to us was that our hearts began to be knit together through the incredible closeness we felt as we prayed to our Father.

Without a counselor to tell us what was wrong, God Himself began to heal our marriage. And with every prayer we prayed together, Jesus became that third strand of a braided cord, binding us tightly together and giving us strength. With this increased spiritual bonding came emotional intimacy. The heart-to-heart connection with my husband that I had desired for so long slowly began to become a reality.

Praying is the sound God's family makes when we are in right relationship with our Lord.

DAVID AND HEATHER KOPP

We've traveled down the road a ways (and made a number of other moves) since we prayed those first halting prayers together on the porch. In the intervening twenty-four years, we've talked to the Lord together about a myriad of concerns. We've prayed our kids through chicken pox, asthma, broken bones, stitches, and painful ear infections. We've asked God such questions as "Where should we send our children to school?" and "Should we sell the house?" We've prayed through business storms, school problems, driver's ed, and prom nights. We've also prayed certain girlfriends and boyfriends out the door—and others in!

We have asked for wisdom when we were fresh out of it, especially when navigating our kids through the rough waters of adolescence. As the years passed, our sphere broadened as we prayed for extended family, friends, missionaries, and others. We've prayed for people who needed

God's love, help, and healing at church and on mission trips. And count-less times we've thanked God for another day of life and for the bounty and blessing of sharing an evening meal or a picnic in the park together as a family.

Sometimes we've talked to the Lord aloud as we drove across the country. Other times we've held hands and prayed silently when there were no words—when both of us lost our parents within a two-year span and as our first grandbaby lay in critical condition in the neonatal intensive care unit. We've knelt to utter innumerable prayers of *I'm sorry, God; I've blown it again.* And more than once we've prayed the "Jehoshaphat" prayer: *Lord, we don't know what to do, but our eyes are upon You.*

We've seen firsthand that praying as a couple *works!* There is a spe-cial effectiveness and power released when ordinary husbands and wives like us agree in prayer. Maybe that's why Satan likes to keep us all so busy that we often have to expend some extra effort to make it happen.

My husband and I have discovered a special, heart-to-heart connec-tion that is only available through prayer and spiritual interaction. When we're fresh out of love and patience with each other, God has an inexhaustible supply of each, ready and waiting for us to ask.

God has taught us a lot through simple prayers uttered over coffee or at our kids' bedsides. And although we've seen Him work in our lives and our children's lives over and over as we've prayed, we still have not arrived. We are still whispering, *Lord, teach us to pray.* And we're still finding that He loves to show us more!

PRAYER EXERCISE
BEGINNINGS

You may be where Holmes and I were when, feeling so estranged, we began the wonderful adventure of praying together. Or maybe you're farther along on your spiritual journey. Talk about where you are right now—both individually and as a couple—with regard to prayer. Maybe, for one of you, disappointment with God blocks the prayer path. Or perhaps you feel disconnected from God. Perhaps you are frustrated because you're busy and going in so many directions that you don't know how to make time for prayer.

Wherever you are, think about where you want to be and what might be the next step for you. Don't worry about not praying in the past. Know that God will accept you right where you are and move you along by His Spirit. All He needs are willing hearts that want to talk and listen to Him!

2

The Ties That Bind

A person standing alone can be attacked and defeated,

but two can stand back-to-back and conquer.

Three are even better,

for a triple-braided cord is not easily broken.

ECCLESIASTES 4:12, NLT

Karen and her husband, Brad, had barely gotten past their eighth anniversary when their relationship hit rock bottom. As is the case in many marriages, the damage didn't happen overnight, but rather accumulated over time. It was a gradual spiral downward.

For years, Brad had worked an almost impossible schedule at his job, which left little time for his family. He never went to church with Karen and their three children, and sometimes the kids didn't see him for days at a time.

Besides being involved with the children's activities and schools, Karen threw herself into a flurry of community and church activities and coached two soccer teams. In an effort to deal with her loneliness and take the edge off her resentment toward her husband's absence and withdrawal, she poured all her energy into things other than her marriage.

Two afternoons a week, when Brad was home, he took care of their youngest child while Karen raced off with the other two to coach their soccer teams. She usually arrived home utterly spent and, after giving the kids their baths and putting them to bed, fell into bed exhausted.

The more Karen invested in outside activities, the more she and Brad went in separate directions. Because they both had resentments over unmet needs, petty irritations erupted into major fights. When they dredged up offenses that the other spouse had committed, their bitterness grew.

After they calmed down, both Brad and Karen would be filled with guilt and regret over the awful things they'd said and about how their fighting upset their kids. They were aware that Satan was pulling them apart and trying to destroy their marriage and that they were cooperating with his schemes, but they didn't know how to get back on course.

Before long, the walls between them seemed too high to scale. Communication became nonexistent, and when they did have a few minutes together without the kids, they didn't enjoy each other. Karen worried that any day she would come home to find a note saying that Brad had filed for divorce. And even if that didn't happen, she was considering leaving him.

Finally an explosive argument pushed them over the edge, and they sought their pastor's help. "Before you do anything, you've got to come together and pray," he pleaded. "Think about your three kids. Just try praying together and see what God might do."

That night Karen and Brad got down on their knees. As they uttered their first words to God in prayer, both began to weep. For the first time in a long time, they felt a surge of compassion for each other. Karen began to see Brad's perspective

> *On the other end of that prayer line is a loving Heavenly Father who has promised to hear and answer our petitions. In this day of disintegrating families on every side, we dare not try to make it on our own.*
>
> JAMES C. DOBSON

instead of just her own. She saw the hurt she'd caused him and the pain that he felt but had trouble acknowledging. She also realized how hard he had been trying to provide for their family by working all those extra hours. She saw his worries about finances.

Brad's heart began to soften toward Karen as well. He sensed how rejected and alone she had felt. In the midst of their prayers and tears, God began healing their marriage.

It didn't happen overnight, but as the couple prayed together in the following days and weeks, God began to fill them with forgiveness for the hurts they had inflicted on each other. Brad learned how to forgive his wife—not just one time, but on a daily basis. As a result, he was no longer held captive by resentment and unforgiveness. His load seemed lighter. Karen felt less alone. When she heard Brad express thanks to God for her and the children, she felt loved and appreciated in a way she had never before experienced.

I seriously doubt if there would be many divorces among Christians if they took time to kneel in prayer once a day and prayed for each other.

RUTH BELL GRAHAM

Each time you forgive your partner you are involved in creating a new beginning in your marriage.

H. NORMAN WRIGHT

Gradually, their hearts were reconnected. In those quiet moments a new intimacy began to develop that warmed their whole relationship and home life.

Soon after that, the couple started praying with their children at bedtime and sharing Scriptures that they had found meaningful or helpful. They both made sacrifices and schedule adjustments in order to spend time together. As they did, Brad and Karen also saw changes in their children. They seemed to fight less. The light was back in their older son's eyes, and his school performance took a leap forward. Recently, his choir director at church remarked to them, "I don't know what you've done, but John Paul is a different child."

Karen and Brad have been praying together for several months now and can hardly believe the renewal their marriage has experienced and the peace God has brought to their family. They believe it wouldn't have happened if they hadn't gotten down on their knees together.

PRAYER EXERCISE

PRAYING FOR YOUR MARRIAGE

From time to time all of us have challenges and roadblocks in our marriages. For Karen and Brad, prayer was the instrument that brought healing.

Think about your biggest problem or the most significant hindrance to the kind of marriage you and your mate would like to have. Maybe it's one spouse's workaholic nature. It could be a deep hurt you've had difficulty forgiving. Perhaps it's the lack of time for communication or a lack of physical intimacy and affection. Pray together and lift those longings and concerns to God. Ask Him for a deeper understanding of each other, for forgiving hearts, and for His Spirit to restore your love for each other.

Remember that because God created the institution of marriage, He desires that *your marriage* succeed and stay the course. When you go to Him for His help in prayer, all of the heavenly resources are available to you.

A Prayer for Our Relationship

Father, our relationship needs healing.
Somehow we've hurt each other, and the distance between us
has grown into a chasm
seemingly too large to leap over by ourselves.
We need You to bridge the gap between the love we've needed
and the love we haven't given each other.
Lord, come with healing in Your wings and touch our hearts!
We need Your forgiveness so we can let go of grievances and love again.
Help us remember that when we get to the end of our human love,
You have an inexhaustible supply of love we can draw upon.
Enable us to be compassionate and humble—
no retaliation or sharp-tongued sarcasm—
and to bless the other.
Let us live out of Your tenderhearted, forgiving love.
Amen.

3

First Love

Rejoice in the wife of your youth.

P R O V E R B S   5 : 1 8 ,   T L B

"*D*o we want a C- marriage or an A+ marriage? Do we want to go on just surviving in a joyless marriage, or do we want to have one that glorifies God and blesses us and our children?"

One night several years ago, Bob and Debby asked each other these questions.

They had been married nine years, and they had four young children, ages seven, five, three, and one. Although they were very committed to their marriage—the word *divorce* wasn't even in their vocabulary—their relationship was going through rough waters.

Bob traveled a great deal. When he was home, he was busy with his ministry, work responsibilities, and other demands. Debby kept a hectic pace at home with the children and all of their activities, and recently she had begun homeschooling their oldest child, Luke. Communication was difficult; times of closeness few and far between. Bob and Debby were beginning to feel more like roommates than husband and wife.

For six months, Debby had struggled with mild depression. She felt that she had lost all the joy in living and in her relationship with Bob. Several sessions of personal and marriage counseling had helped—but now what?

Bob and Debby both knew that prayer was important. Like most busy Christians, they prayed before meals and with their kids at bedtime, while on the run, or whenever a need arose. But having a separate prayer time as a couple had never been a daily priority. Hitting the wall in their marriage, though, was a wake-up call. That night as they talked, Bob and Debby committed to pray together every night. Every night since, even if Bob was on the road, they've joined hearts and talked to God together.

Because Debby was so emotionally drained, Bob did most of the praying in their initial prayer times together. He would kneel beside her and pray that God would heal her depression and restore her joy, that He would give them an A+ marriage, and that He would revive their oneness physically, spiritually, and especially emotionally. Bob's prayers spoke volumes to Debby of his love and com-

Our total couple intimacy is enhanced by our couple prayer. When we listen in to each other's private conversation with God, we are at our most vulnerable. It is a gift we give each other, a special time.

JOEL AND MARIA SHULER

Jesus is knocking on the door of every Christian home, seeking to come in through prayer. He wants to glorify His name through the love, holiness, and unity that He creates in each family.

OLIVER W. PRICE

mitment to her and his desire for their marriage to be not only satisfying and happy, but also to reflect God's glory.

Gradually, as her depression lifted, Debby joined in. They would usually pray after their kids were asleep. If Bob, the early bird, wanted to turn in before Debby was ready for bed, she stopped whatever she was doing so they could pray together. If Bob was out of town, he called and they prayed on the phone. Together, they shared their burdens with the Lord and lifted up concerns about their children. If they knew of needs among family or friends, they prayed for them as well. Sometimes their prayer time lasted twenty minutes. On other nights,

Any couple who develops their capacity to share their spiritual quests is destined to have a triumphant marriage. The two lovers overcome the greatest of all marital enemies—emotional distance. They become joined and merged and blended and interwoven right where they are most wonderfully made—where the spiritual quest happens within them.

NEIL CLARK WARREN

particularly if they were tired, they prayed for only a few minutes, simply thanking God for another day of life and for each other.

As Debby and Bob's spirits connected on a deeper level in prayer, their communication improved dramatically. Their intimate times became sweeter than ever before. They also felt that they were becoming each other's best friend. Out of their prayer times came the idea to have regular date nights and a weekly powwow to communicate what was going on with their children's sports and lessons, Bob's travel schedule, and Debby's activities. Several months later, on their tenth anniversary, they went away by themselves for a weeklong second honeymoon.

Best of all, their romance began to bloom again, and their "first love" for each other is once again burning bright.

Bob still travels three weekends a month speaking and ministering at churches across the country, and their home is as busy as ever. But Bob and Debby's goal is to draw ever closer to God and to keep their hearts connected to each other through daily prayer together. Both agree that their daily prayer time is the foundation and glue of their fourteen-year marriage.

PRAYER EXERCISE
A MONTH OF PRAYERS

Starting today, make a commitment to pray together every day for a month...and watch what happens. Pray about whatever is important to both of you—each other, your kids, jobs, finances, unsaved friends or parents, areas of stress, and needs. For some couples, praying before getting out of bed in the morning is the best time; for others, before going to sleep at night works better. Whatever the time, make it a priority on your daily calendar and stick to it. Like Bob and Debby, you'll find that your efforts result not only in a more satisfying marriage, but also in greater intimacy with God.

Praying with your spouse can be the spark that brings the fire
back into your marriage and spiritual life.
What other activity can foster intimacy, allow you to communicate
your heart and vision, bring about positive changes, and
draw you both closer to God—all at the same time?

DOUG WENDEL

4

Roses in April

Love and faithfulness meet together;

righteousness and peace kiss each other.

Psalm 85:10

od, I think you've called me to marry this girl, but I'm only twenty years old. I haven't finished my degree. You know my heart is to be in ministry. I can't get married now! I've got no money to support a wife.

Bill Farrell argued with God all the way from Bakersfield to his folks' place in Thousand Oaks, where he would be working that summer.

He had met Pam at a student leadership conference, and they started writing each other shortly thereafter. The following winter at another conference, their dating relationship began. This summer they would be separated while Pam attended the Institute for Biblical Studies in Colorado. They had decided to use this time to evaluate their relationship and to pray for God's will to become clear. And they had agreed that they would not talk to each other during this time.

I know how these things work, Lord, Bill reasoned with God. *You get married, your wife gets pregnant, and you have to get a job to make money and work forty years at a job you hate. Surely that's not what You've planned for me. I want to serve You in the ministry, but I need an education. And Lord, I'm too young to get married!*

"Marry her," said a still, small voice.

Logistically, it can't work out, Lord.

"Marry her," Bill seemed to hear again.

There's no way I could get my degree; it just wouldn't work out economically.

As he continued giving God all his excuses, Bill felt a big knot in his stomach. Then he ran out of excuses and grew quiet.

Again Bill sensed God speaking to him: "Marry her."

When Bill finally said, *Okay, okay, Lord, I'll ask her,* peace filled his heart.

But the stark realities of life again overruled his resolve: *Lord, you know I own only two pair of pants—and one of them is ripped at the knee. I don't know how far my blue Vega with the green back door is going to last. I've got a part-time job, but that's not enough to support a wife....*

After two more hours of wrestling, Bill knew the answer: As soon as he and Pam got back together, he would ask her to marry him. As he thought about marrying her, even if it meant that he would have to give up his dream of full-time ministry, he again felt a deep, calming inner sense of peace.

> *Faith is happy to step out not knowing where it's going so long as it knows Who is going along.*
>
> JIM CYMBALA

So from the very beginning, Bill and Pam's marriage was layered with prayer. After a brief engagement, they exchanged vows on Christmas Day. They didn't have much money or material possessions, but they thanked God together at every meal for what they did have, and then kissed. They worked hard—Pam at her college studies and part-time job and Bill at his college studies and full-time job as a draftsman. They both volunteered a combined forty hours a week as junior high and high school ministers at their church. They prayed nightly about their needs and watched God faithfully take care of them.

After their car broke down, they decided to ride bikes so that Bill could concentrate on school instead of taking on extra work to make big car payments every month. Through a series of events that fill their "miracle scrapbook," Bill finished his bachelor's degree in eighteen months. The Lord supplied them with a Chevy Impala for the total sum of $56.17—the cost of a brake job so they could drive it to Los Angeles, where Bill was to attend seminary. Their church and other people helped with financial support the entire time Bill was in seminary. Pam also worked while Bill studied. Through diligence, perseverance, and God's wonderful provision, Bill completed his seminary training and became a pastor.

Thank God you don't have to be flawless to be blessed! You need to have a big heart that desires and wants the will of God more than anything in the world. You need also to have an eye single to His glory.

A . W . TOZER

Bill had not had to give up his dream of being in the ministry. God just had a different way than he did of getting him there. In the process, He did more than Bill or Pam could have asked or thought.

Both Bill and Pam had come from chaotic homes. In the early years of their marriage, they could see that God was helping them develop new habits that would put Him at the center of their home. Their frequent prayer times together gave them a sense of calm, faith, and trust in God's plan for their lives—an essential foundation of strength when they later entered the pastorate, supervised a church building program, and became the parents of three sons.

All seemed well until one morning when Pam woke up feeling that God was speaking to her in a special way. "It was like someone had flipped a switch," Pam reflected later. She felt overwhelmingly that God wanted her to return to school and finish her education, that He wanted her to take their women's ministry to another level, and that He wanted her to begin working on a writing career.

Bill, however, instead of supporting his wife's vision, tried to convince her that her priorities were all wrong. *This isn't the right time,* he thought. *She's manufactured this. Surely it's not a call from God.* Suddenly Pam's dreams were an inconvenience in his life. Her desire to chase her goals put pressure on him to help with domestic duties beyond what Bill thought should be expected of him.

After almost a year of disputes, Pam couldn't say no to the things on her heart, and Bill couldn't say yes. They had reached an impasse.

> *To pray is to change. Prayer is the central avenue God uses to transform us. If we are unwilling to change, we will abandon prayer as a noticeable characteristic of our lives.*
>
> RICHARD FOSTER

They tried every communication technique they'd been taught and had counseled others to do. But everything that had worked before wasn't working anymore. They would schedule a conversation to resolve the issue and then have to reschedule because things would get too heated. They disagreed sharply and couldn't find a middle ground. Finally, Pam and Bill came to the end of themselves. They decided to pray. As they got on their knees by the sofa, both broke down and cried.

God, we know that You know what's best for us, but we're out of options and don't have answers, Bill prayed. *You've been involved in our marriage from the beginning, and You need to either change my heart or Pam's mind, or slow her down. You've got to work and show us how to get through this. If we continue as we are, we're either not going to like each other anymore, or we'll end up as another divorce statistic.*

As the couple prayed their desperate prayers, they placed all their plans and preconceived notions and dreams on the Lord's altar.

Not long after that, something began to change in Bill's heart. Amazingly, he began to see that his wife *couldn't* say no because God had so strongly impressed her with His direction. It was God who had placed this dream in Pam—and he, Bill, was blocking that dream.

Then Bill realized that his argument wasn't with Pam, but with God. As he'd learned early on, he couldn't win an argument with God. However, if he suddenly went to his wife and said, "It's okay. I'm behind you now," she would have a hard time believing him. He had fought her so hard that a simple apology wouldn't be enough.

Heart speaks to heart.

John Henry Newman

Show me, Lord, how I can show Pam that I'll support her. Give me a way to make up for the grief I've caused her, he prayed.

One April day Bill had to be on Pam's campus for a video project he was working on for the church. Pam had a medieval literature class that day, and before she left for class she said, "Think of me when you're on campus today." That's when he got his idea.

"Romance is dead," Pam's professor announced. Leaning against the chalkboard, he went on to enumerate all the reasons why romance was an idealistic fallacy of the Middle Ages that was totally unobtainable today. No one could stay happily married for a lifetime, he told his class. A chorus of women in the room agreed, "Yeah, men are jerks. Romance is dead."

Right in the middle of their vehement tirade against men and romantic love, Bill walked into the room. He walked over to Pam's desk, located inconveniently in the middle of the room, and set down a huge bouquet of a dozen red roses. He then bent down over her left shoulder and whispered, "I love you." With a tender kiss, he left the room as quickly as he'd entered.

"Is this your birthday?" the startled professor asked Pam.

"No."

"Your anniversary?"

"No."

"Then what's the reason? Why did this man come into my class?"

"That's my husband, and I guess he just wanted me to know that he loves me and believes in me!"

Several women chorused, "Does he have a brother?"

The gift of red roses relaid the foundation of trust between Bill and Pam. It would become an anchor point in their love. At first, Bill had not truly believed in his heart that Pam's dream was a calling from God. Eventually his heart caught up, and he cheered her to the finish line. On her graduation day, Bill gathered friends and family, filled the rented recreation hall with helium balloons, and threw Pam a surprise party—complete with a "This Is Your Life!" pageant honoring her life.[2]

As it turned out, Pam was asked to coauthor a book with a well-known couple even before she had finished her degree. Eleven books later, she's still pursuing God's call.

As Bill and Pam learned, when God leads you to do something, it doesn't always make sense. You may not be able to see how it is going to happen.

But God is able and ready to work out His plans for you if you trust Him. Praying together about your dreams gives you the confidence to take the necessary steps even when you can't see how all the pieces fit together.

Maybe you are a couple like Bill and Pam—Bill likes things predictable and planned out, and Pam tends to be spontaneous and passionate. Because they pray together regularly, Bill hears what is on Pam's heart. He has learned that he can trust her to make spontaneous decisions and know that they are God's leading, not merely whims.

Without prayer, it's easy to misinterpret what our spouses do because we don't get a peek into their hearts. God glues our hearts together through prayer and builds a foundation of trust in Him and each other that will last a lifetime.

PRAYER EXERCISE

ANCHOR POINTS

An anchor point is a time when you especially believed in each other or did something so loving that the other will never forget it. Reflect back and talk about one of the anchor points of your relationship. It might be a sacrifice made, a precious surprise, or a random act of romance that melted your heart. Then thank God for this anchor point, for His goodness in giving you each other, and for His faithfulness in keeping you together through disagreements that threatened your harmony.

5

Silent Moments

Who despises the day of small things?

ZECHARIAH 4:10

*A*s you've read the accounts of praying couples in this book, if you've found yourself thinking, *I'd love to see God move in our marriage and family like this, but praying aloud as a couple is not easy or comfortable for us,* I have an encouraging story for you.

When Charlie Shedd, beloved Christian author, and his wife, Martha, were a newly married couple—just a couple of kids fresh from Iowa—one of the first lessons they learned was that there are some things you just can't express in words.

Charlie was studying to be a pastor, and he knew how important prayer and God's Word were for the spiritual bonding he and his young wife desired. But in their first times of prayer together, Martha said that she was afraid that what she said to God would embarrass Charlie.

Charlie understood why she might feel that way. As a seminary student, he was articulate, whether speaking to a group or telling God his thoughts. He sensed that Martha was more than a little intimidated by his verbal skills. So instead of praying aloud, they decided to take a different approach—they began to ask each other about their biggest concerns, listen as each shared, and then pray about them together silently.

Charlie might say, "I'm worried about where our money is going to come from." Martha might add, "I'm worried about our child." Charlie might admit, "I'm concerned that I've been difficult to live with lately." Once they had expressed their concerns, they would hold hands and pray silently for the other person, and then pray the Lord's Prayer together or read Psalm 23 aloud together.

Real life gave this couple many opportunities to join together and pray—when they had a problem they couldn't solve, when they were angry with each other, when they faced financial stresses, or when Charlie wanted to go one direction and Martha wanted to go another.

Another thing that helped their prayer life and brought a closer spiritual bond was their weekly drive. Almost every week, Charlie and Martha would leave the kids with their grandparents or a sitter for an hour or two so they could take a drive together. They'd take along a Bible, and the spouse who wasn't driving would read aloud from a passage they were studying. Then they

---

Real success in life, and in marriage, comes only when a couple unites together in the Lord and serves Him together.

C H A R L I E   S H E D D

The intimate sharing and the deep connecting of prayer together are like the cream of a marriage.

In prayer we can have the intimate knowledge of the shape of one another's souls.

V A L E R I E   A N D   S T E V E   B E L L

---

would talk, share prayer concerns, and pray silently.

They found other ways to share God's Word together. Sometimes they chose one verse of the Bible as their verse for the day and "wrote it on their hearts" in the morning. That night before going to bed, they told each other what their verse was and what it meant to them. In forty-eight years of marriage they read through the Bible twenty-two times, discussing their questions and insights along the way.

As the Shedds grew in their marriage and in Christ, Martha's self-consciousness gradually melted away, and they were able to pray aloud together. Like all of us, at times they had needs that they didn't know how to verbalize— so they would go back to praying together silently. But whether praying aloud or silently, they treasured their prayer times together and the "soul harmony" that resulted.[3]

But in our silent moments in God's presence, silent moments so full of truth, love, and respect for others, a second movement of the soul can bring us to overcome this holding back of ourselves which took over so quickly and which could again jeopardize our marital oneness. Because of such moments we have come to experience much more than a wonderful marriage; we have come, through each other, to experience God himself.

PAUL TOURNIER

Couples around them were so struck by the happiness in the Shedds' marriage that they asked if Charlie and Martha could help them deal with their problems and develop better marriages. And so began their marriage ministry, which eventually blessed thousands and thousands of families around the world.

PRAYER EXERCISE
SILENT MOMENTS

Find a few quiet moments together when you can be alone. Sit knee-to-knee and express your most pressing concerns or needs to your spouse. Then hold hands and pray silently for each other's burden. Conclude by reading a psalm together or praying the Lord's Prayer aloud.

Inspired by the example of Charlie and Martha Shedd, here are some other things you might try to develop spiritual intimacy:

- Take a drive or, when you travel together, devote the first half hour to the passenger reading aloud from Proverbs, Psalms, or another favorite book of the Bible.
- Keep a One-Year Bible in your car for when you are traveling or running errands together. Have the passenger read a portion of the day's Scripture.
- In your individual Bible reading, choose one verse as your verse for the day; write it out on a three-by-five-inch card, and meditate on it throughout the day. Then, before going to bed, share with your spouse what your verse was and what it meant to you.
- Try a weekly "word focus." Think of one of the greatest needs in your marriage—maybe it's patience or joy or servanthood or another quality. Look up the word in the dictionary, and then go to a concordance and find Bible verses on the subject. Choose one of those verses to focus on in the following week, and share with your spouse any way the verse touches your life or how it is becoming a part of you. The following week, choose a different need in your marriage and a word to reflect it. Continue this for a month, sharing your discoveries with each other and thanking God for what He is revealing to you.

A Prayer for God's Help

Father, we come to You as children who aren't very good
at this prayer thing.
We feel awkward, self-conscious, and inadequate
to talk to You aloud together.
So we ask You: Please teach us to pray!
Help us to open our hearts to You and each other.
Give us grace to be honest and transparent.
Dissolve our fears and insecurities with Your love.
Most of all, help us get our focus off of ourselves and
onto You when we pray.
Show us Scriptures we can pray back to You
so we'll be praying in Your will.
And help us make prayer a natural part of our lives like eating,
breathing, and talking.
Amen.

6

Mentored in Prayer

"We will give ourselves continually to prayer."

ACTS 6:4, NKJV

As a newlywed twenty-one years ago, Jennifer was determined that she would be the perfect wife and that she and her husband, Wayne, would have the "perfect marriage." Prayer as a couple was central to her plan. So imagine her dismay when she discovered that praying together, instead of being natural and open, was uncomfortable, stilted, and forced.

For Jennifer, who was experienced at it, nothing was more open and honest than prayer. But that was just the problem. She could pour out her heart to God in private, but she discovered that she wasn't yet ready to reveal her true self to Wayne in the way that whole-souled prayer requires. So when they prayed together, she tended to edit her thoughts and feelings.

Wayne, on the other hand, had prayed aloud only in formal church settings. Knowing his wife's passion for prayer, he sensed that Jennifer would have expectations he could not meet. As a result, he felt self-conscious and inadequate while praying with his new wife.

Even though it was awkward, the couple kept muddling through. They knew that praying together was crucial to the kind of home they hoped to create. They wanted to stay close to God and each other—to be unified in their spiritual life. But they found it easier to talk about their prayers than to actually pray together.

The turning point for this couple came through a small-group experience. Wayne and Jennifer joined a home Bible study and prayer group that met weekly. It turned out that they were the youngest group members. Another couple, John and Margaret, had grown children and several grandchildren.

Without really intending to, John and Margaret became role models of prayer for Wayne and Jennifer. They were genuine, warm, and at ease with each other as they prayed almost as one—Margaret's prayers blending into John's and his into hers—both praying conversationally and with hearts wide open to God.

As the group shared burdens and prayed for one another, Wayne

Our God, an intimate God, has designed us to relate to Him with the person who is most intimate with us. If we expect to colabor as husband and wife in the work God has given each of us, then we need also to communicate with Him as a couple.

DOUG WENDEL

Prayer is...love's tender dialogue between the soul and God.

JOHN RICHARD MORELAND

and Jennifer gradually began to feel more comfortable praying aloud. Perhaps learning to pray together with a group took some of the pressure off. And certainly John and Margaret's wonderful example helped the younger couple see that couple prayer could be a natural, joyful experience.

This was Wayne and Jennifer's launching pad. The comfort they'd found praying in the group extended into their prayer life at home. In the months that followed, as they prayed together about direction and saw God open doors, or as they prayed for neighbors and acquaintances and saw God create opportunities to minister, their enthusiasm for praying together increased. When life's inevitable difficulties came along, they had a way to go before God with one heart and mind as they worked through their problems.

Spiritual intimacy is the satisfying connectedness that occurs when a husband and wife learn to access God and experience Him together on the deepest levels.

VALERIE AND STEVE BELL

Prayer is opening ourselves to God so that He can open us to others.

LOUIS EVELY

Although their twenty-one-year marriage has had its rough spots, Wayne and Jennifer have always found their way back to prayer—and through prayer, they've found unity. After a slow, awkward start, praying together is now the mainstay of their marriage.

PRAYER EXERCISE
CONVERSATIONAL PRAYER

If praying together is awkward or uncomfortable for you, join a small group. It could be a small Bible study, a "connections" or cell group from your church, or a couples prayer group. By learning to pray conversationally in a group setting and being mentored by others more experienced at prayer, you can ease into praying as husband and wife just as Wayne and Jennifer did.

When you do pray as a twosome, use a *conversational style,* praying back and forth over one issue in short one- or two-sentence prayers before moving on to the next topic. Neither of you should feel pressured to pray long prayers or cover all the bases of a topic, because the Holy Spirit can weave your petitions together. At first, try praying for a short period of time, and then gradually increase your prayer time as you become more comfortable together in God's presence.

Be patient with yourself and your spouse—it may take some time before praying as a couple becomes natural. But it will yield long-lasting, eternal rewards.

7

Making the Connection

I thank my God every time I remember you....

I always pray with joy because of your partnership

in the gospel from the first day until now.

PHILIPPIANS 1:3–5

On Les and Leslie Parrott's wedding day, they made a commitment to one another: They would pray for each other every day, whether they were together or separated due to work or ministry in other cities.

Because of a simple promise made years ago, they have now prayed daily for each other's needs for sixteen years. They've been surprised at how much they've appreciated their mate's prayers for the commonplace challenges of life: for resolution of a conflict with a best friend...for the decisions to be made about an ill mother's care...for wisdom to teach their university classes or to counsel a married couple or a troubled student...and most importantly, for keeping them connected while one of them was traveling.

Sharing their prayer times didn't come naturally to this couple. In some ways, Les and Leslie are opposites, so they have struggled to find time and a way to pray together consistently. Les, for example, is a late-night person, while Leslie likes to pray early in the morning. One of them might be all set to pray, but the other might not be in the mood. Les has an intellectual style of connecting with God that needs the stimulation of analyzing Scripture, whereas Leslie has a more contemplative style. She needs quiet devotional time to listen to the Lord and seems to connect best with Him as she enjoys nature.

Despite their differences, their commitment to pray stimulated Les and Leslie to search for creative ways to share their spiritual lives, and they've come up with many ideas that have worked for both of them. For example, they may go on a hike and then read a Psalm praising God's marvelous creation. They also avoid making the other feel guilty if one of them doesn't want to pray at a particular time.

Along the way, Les and Leslie have kept their commitment to pray for each other daily. A few years ago, this promise made all the difference for their family. For fourteen years, they had deeply desired a child, and when Leslie finally became pregnant, they were thrilled. Her pregnancy, however, was a tough one.

A little more than halfway into it, doctors sent Leslie to the hospital for complete bed rest. Although the couple tried to cancel or reschedule their

What marvelous power there is in prayer! What untold miracles it works in this world! What untold benefits does it secure to those who pray!

E. M. BOUNDS

When the two of you begin to regularly lift up each other's cares in prayer, you will see not only benefits in your communication but also power answers wrought by the Hand of God.

BILL AND LYNDI MCCARTNEY

numerous speaking engagements, many of them could not be changed, so Les, deeply concerned about his wife and baby, had to meet them alone.

On one such weekend, Leslie prayed for her husband as he headed for the airport. And Les prayed for her, asking for wisdom for the doctors who carefully monitored the health of Leslie and their unborn baby. With the due date so far away, they felt pretty safe that it wouldn't be a crisis weekend. But it was still difficult for Les to leave and for Leslie to be alone in the hospital.

As she lay there, hooked up to monitors, Leslie asked God to sustain her husband, to give him wisdom and the words he needed to speak. She prayed for special peace for Les because she knew that he hated to leave and would be devastated if anything happened in his absence. Throughout the weekend, even though she wasn't aware of weather conditions and felt too sick even to watch the news on TV, she felt led to pray for traveling mercies and for her husband's plane to return on time.

As white snow flakes fall quiet and thickly on a winter day, answers to prayer will settle down upon you at every step you take.... The story of your life will be the story of prayer and answers to prayer.

O. HALLESBY

As Les flew from Seattle to North Carolina for the speaking engagements, he earnestly prayed for the well-being of his wife and unborn son, John. He and Leslie had both been hoping and praying that John would make it to the twenty-eighth week, when his lungs would be developed to the point that he would have a chance for survival. That morning, Les felt even more urgency to pray for the baby's lungs. He also prayed that he would be with his wife when his son was born.

And Lord, please give Leslie the peace that passes all understanding, he prayed over and over. Though separated by several thousand miles, the couple held each other up in prayer during those two days.

On Sunday the doctor checked Leslie. With a note of urgency that took Leslie by surprise, he said, "We've got to deliver this baby. We have about four more hours before your body shuts down completely."

Alone, and too ill to pick up the phone and ask her mother or their church members to pray or to come be with her, Leslie was prepped for the delivery room. Normally, she would have felt panicked at being alone in such a crisis. Yet an extraordinary peace settled into her heart—a precious gift from God and an answer to her husband's prayers.

There is no more significant involvement in another's life than prevailing, consistent prayer. It is more helpful than a gift of money, more encouraging than a strong sermon, more effective than a compliment, more reassuring than a physical embrace.

CHUCK SWINDOLL

Meanwhile, severe winter storms on the East Coast grounded many planes, including Les's. However, a kind ticket agent found him a different flight from Charlotte to Seattle, and he arrived there on schedule. He drove home unaware of what was going on at the hospital and even took time to shower before he went to see Leslie.

When Les got to the hospital, he learned that his wife would go into delivery in one hour and forty minutes.

As Leslie was wheeled to the delivery room, Les walked alongside the gurney, holding her hand even as he grabbed the phone to marshal prayer support from friends and family.

Baby John was born on the first day of his twenty-eighth week—a miraculous survival. And Dad was there with Mom to welcome him with all the love in their hearts. Since he was two months premature and weighed only a pound and a half, little John had to survive many challenges during the first months of his life, first in the neonatal intensive care unit, and then at home.

John is now a toddler, and Les and Leslie's home is an even busier place. Although their teaching and speaking schedules still keep them apart at times, they keep their commitment to pray for each other every day. And as they do, God continues to bless their lives by making them more and more the soul mates He intended them to be.

PRAYER EXERCISE

PREVAILING, CONSISTENT PRAYER FOR YOUR SPOUSE

Making a commitment to pray for your spouse daily may be one of the most enriching and spiritually bonding things you can do for your marriage. Keep in touch with each other's needs by asking, "What are the major concerns you have today or this week? What is causing you stress? What are you most burdened or excited about?"

Lift these things up to God in prayer as you go about your day. And be sure to check in and tell each other how God is meeting the needs you're both praying about. You'll be amazed at how He knits your hearts together as you pray faithfully for one another.

8

A Symphony of Prayer

God has given each of you some special abilities;

be sure to use them to help each other,

passing on to others God's many kinds of blessings.

1 PETER 4:10, TLB

After supper, Maria cleaned up the kitchen while her husband, Jeff, enthusiastically welcomed his friends into the living room for their Thursday night prayer meeting.

"So glad you're here, Don. Come on in!"

"Thanks for having us every week, Jeff."

"Hey—this is the highlight of my week!" Jeff responded. "Hi, Jack! Glad you're here."

Every week the men met and prayed what they called "God's Agenda." They earnestly interceded for revival, for leaders, and for their own lives and careers. They shared their hopes and concerns, their fears and vulnerabilities. Their prayer time created a great sense of intimacy and closeness.

Over time, Jeff became a little disturbed that he felt more bonded spiritually with his friends than with his own wife. Maria was frustrated as well. Whenever she heard Jeff and his friends talking and praying together, she thought, *I'm glad Jeff enjoys praying with the guys, but I wish I were included.*

Nevertheless, when they did try to pray together, their attempts ended in frustration and even resentment. Jeff criticized Maria's prayers; she, in turn, corrected his grammar! Other differences compounded the problem: Jeff prayed for justice and correction; Maria for mercy and compassion. She liked to pray with the lights off; he preferred the lights on. Maria prayed from her heart and emotions; Jeff analyzed things and wanted to make sure their prayers were in line with Scripture. And worst of all, he continued to correct her prayers.

> *If we can understand and put these different gifts to work, God will be blessed, the enemy crippled, and the family united in powerful prayer.*
>
> ALICE SMITH

When they prayed for a friend in crisis, Maria said, *Lord, I know Jim has a good heart. Please help him.*

"How can you say you know he has a good heart?" Jeff challenged her. "Only God knows a man's heart."

Maria's gift of compassion filled her petitions with a desire for others to experience God's grace and comfort in a time of trial. *Dear Jesus, scoop up Jane and Gary in Your arms and show them Your love,* she prayed when some friends were having terrible financial problems.

She just doesn't understand the whole story; she doesn't realize what really needs to be prayed, Jeff thought. *God, help Jane and Gary buck up and follow Your commands. Correct them and show them they're doing the wrong thing—and how to follow the right principles,* he prayed.

On another occasion, Maria interceded for a friend, *O Lord, Carolyn is a trophy of your grace.*

"What a cliché," Jeff said. "What on earth is a 'trophy of God's grace'?"

They were more like prayer adversaries than prayer partners. Maria grew to intensely dislike praying with Jeff, and little by little, feeling that he was rejecting her heart, she withdrew from him. Despite their prayer times together, their marriage seemed to be dying.

When a marriage course was offered at their church, Jeff and Maria decided to take it. There, Jeff learned not to crush his wife with criticism or correction when she was opening her heart to God.

He also learned that a wife brings different gifts and different pieces of the puzzle to prayer and to life. The fact that his wife might pray about things he hadn't considered or get a picture in her mind's eye while praying wasn't evidence of biblical ignorance or of an overly active imagination. Jeff's prayers weren't superior just because God spoke to him primarily through Scripture passages. Their differences were part of God's design.

We all have different gifts. We can either blend together like a professional symphony or clash like a junior high band...these amazing gifts promise to color and enhance our prayer life in a fun and creative way.

A RT H UNT

For the first time, Jeff began to realize that if he would listen closely and hear the things on his wife's heart, he would gain a special treasure. He came to understand that her gentle spirit and gifts of compassion and discernment were blessings from God.

Maria knew things were changing when Jeff asked her to pray with him about a new job opportunity. The company he worked for had offered him a significant promotion, but it would mean a transfer from the corporate office to the refining division. Although he was leaning toward accepting the offer, he couldn't shake a restless feeling in his spirit.

As they prayed together, Maria's mind formed a mental picture of a vine with many branches. Through this picture, she sensed that the Lord might be saying that Jeff should stay close to the vine and not get out on the branches. Somewhat skeptically, Jeff received this as direction to remain in the corporate office. He declined the promotion and transfer, but he couldn't help wondering if he had made a bad career decision.

Shortly thereafter, Jeff received a promotion within his department. At the same time the corporate office announced its decision to sell the refining division. When refining was sold, many managers at the refinery lost their jobs. Would he have lost his? Jeff didn't know. Did he make a bad career decision or a good one? He still didn't know. But that wasn't the point. He *did* know that he had gained respect for his wife's unique prayer gifts and had great peace about that decision.

Intimacy requires growing transparency. I let go of some of my defenses in order to let the other see me as I am.

WILLIAM BARRY

As they prayed together more often, Jeff began to regard Maria's role as the "radar" and his as the "air force." With her spiritual radar, Maria could readily see what was on the horizon; Jeff could then join her, praying in agreement with her as he went into action in spiritual warfare. Instead of thinking that Maria worried too much, he began to see that his wife's concern over a problem was like a blip on the radar screen alerting them that a special prayer effort was needed. As Jeff's ability to respond to the blips improved, Maria's tuning and discernment improved as well.

Maria would often come home burdened for one of the students in her Earth Science class—parents divorcing, family members injured or dying, brothers or sisters having problems—all of which showed up in poor grades, rebellion, or being distracted during class. Now, instead of ignoring her or criticizing her caring spirit, Jeff took the cue and joined her in intercession for her students.

Once, one of her students was struggling with school and friends because her dad was dying of cancer. Maria was concerned that the young girl would be derailed academically for years as a result of poor learning. As she and Jeff prayed together, God gave them specific targets—that the girl and her mother would support each other and that the girl would not become bitter toward God for taking her father.

As Jeff grew to appreciate Maria more, and as they accepted each other's gifts and differences, Maria's heart warmed to her husband, and she looked forward to their times of praying as a couple. By learning to pray together in harmony, their love and intimacy grew deeper. As they looked to God as the conductor and harmonized together in prayer, they became part of His grand symphony of intercession and saw Him move in dynamic ways not only in the lives of others, but also in their marriage.

How can the two be brought together? We can...ask God to lead us there, to show us the way himself, to bring about this total unity which is, according to his plan, to be the experience of marriage.

PAUL TOURNIER

PRAYER EXERCISE
BLENDING YOUR PRAYER STYLES

Sit down with your spouse and talk about your different gifts, prayer styles, and approaches to prayer. Maybe one of you likes to use a prayer list, while the other likes to feel led by the Spirit. Perhaps one of you is more emotional and prays heartfelt prayers, while the other is more analytical. Matthew 18:19 promises, "Again I tell you, if two of you on earth agree (harmonize together, make a symphony together) about whatever [anything and everything] they may ask, it will come to pass and be done for them by My Father in heaven" (AMP).

Whatever your prayer styles, accept each other's differences. Realize that if God wanted you to pray exactly the same way with the same style and gifts, you wouldn't need each other! Discussing your differences and thanking God for them is a first step toward melding them in prayer.

In the spirit of Matthew 18:19, invite the Holy Spirit to blend your different prayer styles together into a beautiful symphony led by God Himself. Ask Him to bring you together in unity and to use your prayer times to help accomplish His purpose.

A Prayer for Harmony

Father, thank You for meeting us just where we are
but loving us too much to leave us there!
Thank You for constantly working within us to will
and to do Your good pleasure
and to conform us to the image of Christ.
We are so different, Lord—our gifts, our ways of praying
and doing so many things.
Sometimes we feel like polar opposites.
Give us understanding so we will appreciate Your handiwork in the other,
realizing that each of us is fearfully and wonderfully made,
wired for Your purposes and designed uniquely to complement the other.
Show us how to blend together into Your harmony
as we pray, live, parent, and work together.
Make us an effective prayer team so that, together,
we can bring our family, neighbors,
and others to Your throne of grace and You will be glorified.
Amen.

9

Tuning In

Submit to one another

out of reverence for Christ.

Ephesians 5:21

For years, Mike and Harriet McManus have prayed together before starting their day. They first realized their need to have a daily meeting with God and each other at a Marriage Encounter weekend in 1976. Praying together that weekend was so meaningful that they wanted to continue. But they found it difficult because their kids were small, and once they got up, the household was a whirlwind of activity. By the time they returned home, Mike and Harriet knew that they would have to get up earlier, before their boys tumbled out of bed.

So from then on, around 6:15 A.M. they read a psalm or Scripture passage, opened their hearts to God and each other, and prayed. They talked about their hopes and worries and prayed for each other's concerns. They also prayed for their sons—for their current needs as well as for their future spouses and for God's direction for their lives. In this very concrete way, they put Christ at the center of their marriage and family.

In the spring of 1987, Mike sensed the need to move from their Connecticut home to the Washington, D.C., area. A syndicated columnist, he needed to be close to the center of things in the nation's capital. As a family, they could be closer to Harriet's parents, who were both in their eighties. To Mike, moving seemed a wise thing for them to do.

But Harriet strongly disagreed. She loved the house they lived in. She had spent years restoring and decorating it to make a home where their family could thrive. Her biggest worry was their son, who was entering ninth grade. If their house didn't sell until sometime during the school year, the move could be very disruptive at a crucial time in the boy's life.

Jesus' love toward us is free and unmerited.... And He waits only for one thing, and for this He must wait, and that is for us to ask Him to help us. For Jesus will not and cannot force Himself into our distress. We ourselves must open unto Him. And that is the only purpose that our prayers should serve.

O. HALLESBY

"Let's pray about it," Mike suggested one morning during their quiet time. He didn't want to force his will on his wife or coerce or nag her into something she was opposed to. They both believed in the value of submitting to each other in reverence to Christ (Ephesians 5:21) and would not commit to anything until they were of one mind about the decision.

Harriet felt Mike's strong love. She knew that he was sure of his reasons for the move, and she appreciated the fact that he didn't try to pressure her to accept them. Mike was willing to give up his desires to wait for God's timing—willing to wait until they were in agreement. So each morning in March, they lifted the matter up to God and prayed for Him to show the way.

In April, Mike proposed putting the house on the market at a very high price—well over market value. If the house didn't sell by August, they would take it off the market. That way their son wouldn't have to pull up roots in the middle of his first year in high school. On the other hand, a profit would help with their two older sons in college, and if the Lord provided a buyer at that price, they would view that as His confirmation of the move. *Would Harriet agree?* Mike wondered. After some discussion of his plan, she was ready, and the house went up for sale.

All spring and summer there was no action on the house. Then in August, at what seemed the very last minute, a buyer offered the price they were asking. Mike and Harriet had just enough time to find a home in Maryland before school started. The substantial amount they made on the house not only compensated for the investment of time and money Harriet had put into their home, but it also helped them finance many of their sons' college expenses. As He answered their prayers, God also worked in their relationship—both were now in full agreement that the move was the best thing for their family.

Only two months after they had settled in Maryland, the stock market crashed, and prices of houses in the metropolitan New York City/Connecticut area plummeted in the wake of Black Monday. Homes

> *If your day is hemmed with prayer, it is less likely to unravel.*
>
> ANONYMOUS

> *Being able to bow in prayer as the day begins or ends gives expression to the frustrations and concerns that might otherwise not be ventilated.*
>
> JAMES DOBSON

in their former neighborhood dropped in value by as much as 100,000 dollars.

To Mike and Harriet, the entire transition was a demonstration of the perfection of God's ways. His timing had been perfect, and because the couple had submitted the issue to Him, respected each other's perspective, and prayed about it together, God had enhanced their marriage and made their love grow even stronger.

PRAYER EXERCISE

INVITING JESUS IN

Most couples faithfully tune in to the TV news to keep up with what's going on in our world, but too many of us fail to tune in to our partner and the Lord. Jesus stands at the door knocking, gives a warm invitation, and waits for us to open the door. How wonderful when, as a couple, we invite Him in to shine His light on our day! When decisions need to be made, we can submit them to each other and to God and ask Him to bring our hearts into agreement with His will and purpose.

Mike and Harriet minister to many couples through their ministry, Marriage Savers. They suggest that couples view their home as a small, Christ-centered church by studying God's Word, worshiping Him, and praying for each other on a daily basis. Whether you need to rise fifteen minutes earlier in the morning or reserve time before bed, make quiet time together your top priority every day.

An Orphan in Distress

The Christian who is pure and without fault,

from God the Father's point of view,

is the one who takes care of orphans and widows.

JAMES 1:27, TLB

*D*ee and Steve Brestin's sons had already flown the nest, and it wouldn't be long before their teenage daughters took flight as well. Dee and her husband were entering a new phase of life—or so she thought.

"I think we should adopt again, Dee," Steve remarked over dinner one night. The couple had adopted their youngest daughter, Annie, from Korea several years before.

His comment had come out of the blue. *Is he joking?* Dee wondered.

"The overseas orphanages are teeming with children. Let's call Holt International and tell them we're ready for a challenge: an older child, maybe, or a handicapped child, or a sibling group," Steve continued. "Besides, we're finally getting good at parenting—why should we stop now?"

Dee was speechless. *He's serious!*

Dee definitely was not as enthusiastic about rescuing an orphan as her husband was. "I don't think so," Dee finally said.

"Honey, would you be willing to pray about it?"

She paused a long time before she answered, "Well...okay."

"Great! Let's go into the living room right now and kneel before God. Let's try to get rid of our own desires and seek His desire."

When Dee and Steve knelt to pray and listen to God, she didn't hear anything. No telling Scripture verses came to mind. No strong impression came to her heart. Just silence. After what seemed like a long time, she looked up. Her husband had a stunned look on his face.

Where does love begin?

In our own homes.

When does it begin?

When we pray together.

MOTHER TERESA

"What is it?" she asked.

"Oh, maybe I just imagined it."

"Imagined what?" Dee asked.

"While we were praying, I saw a young girl crying. And then I was reminded of that verse in James about how true religion—what really pleases God—is taking care of widows and orphans."

Dee was quiet. She knew Steve wasn't given to hearing voices or seeing visions. He was a competent orthopedic surgeon who was practical, serious, and steady in his walk with God and his leadership of their family.

Finally Steve stood up. "Let's just wait a few days and see how God works."

A few days later the phone rang. It was Barbara Kim, who worked with Holt International Children's Services and had just returned from an orphanage in Bangkok, Thailand. "Dee, we have chosen twelve children out of five hundred from that orphanage—children who have spirits of survival. There was one little girl who stole our hearts—and several of us thought of your family."

"Why us?" Dee inquired.

"She reminded us of your oldest daughter. Like Sally, Beth is charming and winsome. All that's wrong with her is that she's missing an arm. It was amputated, and she was abandoned as a baby. She's almost ten years old. Could we send you her picture? Would you be willing to pray?"

"Okay," Dee replied hesitantly, "send the picture and we'll pray." She still resisted the thought of adopting another child. But could God be up to something?

When the envelope arrived, Dee propped it on the dinner table and waited for Steve to come home. She prayed. She paced. Finally her husband arrived and, with trembling hands, opened the envelope. A picture of a beautiful young girl fell out, and he stared at her face. "Dee, this is the little girl whose face I saw when we prayed!"

Dee's heart froze. Didn't God know that she already had a full plate—parenting their teenagers, teaching a Bible study, and a full schedule of speaking and writing commitments? How could she possibly have time for another child, especially one with special needs? *Doesn't God care about me and my life?* she thought.

Prayer moves God, and when God moves in your life, things get exciting!

JONI EARECKSON TADA

But Dee and Steve continued to pray. She asked close friends to pray for her concerning her quest for peace about adopting Beth. Gradually, God began to reveal attitudes that were hindering His will: fear, lack of mercy, and even embarrassment over the idea that Beth had to do some daily tasks with her feet and her teeth. As Dee confessed her attitudes and asked God to change her heart, His grace began to flow. Part of that grace was her friend Janet, who told Dee that if they adopted the child, she would love to help. She even offered to tutor Beth in English in her home every day.

Steve and Dee decided to go for it. The adoption journey wasn't easy. Countless times they knelt boldly before the Lord, asking Him to tame a new lion that had sprung onto their path. But finally the day arrived when they flew to Thailand to meet their new ten-year-old daughter and settle all the paperwork with the authorities.

They will never forget Beth's radiant face when they met her at the orphanage. This was a child who, at the time Steve and Dee had prayed, had given up hope of ever having a home. They were overwhelmed to realize that God had heard her cry. Now Beth would have a home with loving Christian parents, sisters and brothers, a church community to love and support her, a future, and a hope.

Beth is now in her early twenties. Her transition to a new country and family wasn't without its bumps. Due to the wounds in her early life, Beth came into the family with some emotional walls that seemed insurmountable. But gradually the barriers are falling away. She has received Christ and is growing spiritually. Although she initially struggled with English, she is a hard

To love does not mean simply to look at one another but to look together in the same direction.

ANTOINE DE SAINT-EXUPÉRY

Prayer that leads a couple increasingly to the heart of God is prayer worth making time for, even in the most demanding and pressed of schedules.

CAREY MOORE AND
PAMELA ROSEWELL MOORE

worker and a straight-A student. And she has a smile that warms the coldest of hearts.

Steve and Dee are seeing real fruit in the life of their daughter, who was once an orphan in distress. Beth found true hope when a husband and wife prayed together, listened to God's heart, and obeyed His leading for the sake of one of His little ones.

PRAYER EXERCISE
WHEN YOU ARE ON DIFFERENT PAGES

Is there a course of action that God seems to be speaking about to you or your mate, but that one of you is resisting because it seems difficult or undesirable? If so, commit to praying together about it. Ask God to clarify His will for both of you and to reveal any attitudes that may be preventing your agreement or obedience. As He did with Dee, God will work in your hearts so you can truly be of one mind.

Team Meeting

In the morning I lay my requests before you.

PSALM 5:3

Consistency in their prayer life together? *Impossible,* Pam thought.

Rich and Pam had four young children, all born within six years. They had maintained a daily prayer time before the kids came along, but with kids, it was hard to find any regular time to pray. Dominated by nursing babies, getting up in the night, fatigue, and multiple demands on their time, their schedule changed constantly.

Although they managed a hurried prayer here and there, they both had a heartfelt desire to go deeper. They longed for time to read the Bible together, share, and pray. But without a plan, the days just kept slipping by.

Finally, Rich and Pam decided to assess their body clocks. That appeared to be one of their main obstacles. Rich, a night owl, preferred praying before going to bed. Pam, however, was exhausted late at night. A morning person, she preferred to pray early in the day. As they analyzed and tweaked their schedules, they finally came up with a prayer plan that worked for them despite these differences.

Pam rises at 5:45 A.M., puts on a pot of coffee, and attacks the tread-mill in the basement, allowing Rich an extra hour of sleep. At 6:45, while Pam takes a quick shower, Rich stumbles out of bed, picks up the morning newspaper, and brings the coffee and paper up to their bedroom.

Meeting back on the bed, coffee cups in hand, they begin their team meeting with each other and God. First they review their individual schedules for the day. On some days they then read a short segment in a devotional book; on others they share Bible verses from a Scripture reading program. They vary their readings to help keep these morning times fresh.

God's purpose in marriage isn't meeting your needs. It's meeting His needs. He's the Owner and Coach! That's why you need to be a team.

WELLINGTON BOONE

We cannot sit around waiting for God to "zap" us. We must do what we can to put ourselves in situations where God can speak to us and change us.

LEN WOODS

Finally they go before God in prayer. Rich and Pam both pray as they feel led. They recognize and thank the Lord for who He is and what He has done in their lives. They bring their family and business concerns to Him. This helps to reinforce their goal of being a team in the face of the pressures of the outside world.

Rich and Pam feel that their team prayer time jump-starts their day and helps keep their focus on the Lord. It's a sweet time of communication between Pam, Rich, and God as they pray about many things—big and small, usual and unusual, but all significant to them as a couple. If they're lucky, they finish before the door flies open and four energetic children charge in and jump on the bed. If they're still praying, the kids get to listen in as their parents lift up their biggest concerns to God and pray blessings on each other and on each child.

Some of this couple's most important team meetings focused on whether they should uproot their family of six so that Rich could take a new job. When they had moved into their storybook community outside Chicago, Pam had already relocated several times, and she told herself that this was the *last move*. They were living in her dream English Tudor house and were highly involved in a top-rated school system, where the kids were excelling. Pam and Rich loved the church they attended, and their children ran freely in the safe neighborhood. Nearby were dear friends who felt like family. This was the perfect neighborhood and house. It was where they belonged, and Pam couldn't picture them being anywhere else.

Jesus Christ is not the slave of numbers. He is there wherever faithful hearts meet, however few they may be, for He gives all of Himself to each individual person.

William Barclay

So when a company in Denver began phoning and pursuing Rich, Pam wouldn't even pray about the new job opportunity. If they moved, they could end up in a bad school situation or be next to a house with kids who would have a negative influence on their children. A move meant leaving their extended family. She wondered how God could provide anything more fulfilling than what they had in their comfortable Chicago suburb. Why would they want to leave?

As the mornings went by and the couple held their team meetings with God, Pam would not budge. For six months she wouldn't even look at the company's information packet. Even when the family went to Denver for a family trip, she wouldn't let Rich stop in the company's parking lot or go inside to check things out.

"They called me again today…," Rich told her one day.

"Oh no! What do they want this time?" Pam replied. She continued to be adamantly opposed to the idea.

Let prayer be the key of the morning and the bolt at night.

UNKNOWN

Nevertheless, she heard the excitement in her husband's voice, and little by little she realized that it could be a good opportunity for him. God gradually softened her heart to the point that she prayed, although reluctantly, about the possibility of a move.

Then one day she picked up the information packet. As she read about the company, the area, and the community church, she felt a twinge of excitement. She thought, *Maybe there could be another place where God could meet our needs.* To her surprise, the Lord opened her mind and heart and made her willing to fly to Denver with Rich to check things out.

One step led to another, and a few months later the family moved to Denver. There were some transitions and obstacles, of course, but Rich has flourished in his new responsibilities. He and Pam continuously thank God for His numerous blessings: a beautiful two-year-old home with unobstructed views of the Rockies; an excellent school system; a fenceless, "run free" neighborhood; and good friends from the kids' school living right next door. They have found a wonderful church with a mature and godly staff. God threw in an extra blessing by providing enthusiastic and caring neighbors…from Chicago! Rich and Pam don't feel so far from the Windy City when they can reminisce about it. Today Pam can honestly say that she and Rich wouldn't want to be anywhere else.

When Pam reflects back on those particular team meetings with her husband, she wonders what her life would have been like now if she hadn't taken those tiny steps of faith that enabled her to pray about the possibility of moving.

PRAYER EXERCISE
YOUR OWN TEAM MEETING

Talk with God about your schedules and your individual body clocks, and then experiment with different times to hold your team meeting. Whether you pray together in the car as you drive, after dinner, or in the quiet of the early morning when your kids are still asleep, let communication with each other and with the Lord be your top priority of the day. Remember, wherever or whenever your team meeting is, He will be there with you.

A Prayer for Unity

Lord, we desperately need Your mercy and grace today.
We just can't agree on this issue.
In fact, both of us have entirely different ways of looking at it!
We ask You to bring our minds and hearts into agreement
with each other and with Your will.
Help us to see Your bigger plan instead of focusing on our small agenda
and to submit to each other out of reverence to Christ.
Give us Your thoughts and perspective as we lay down ours.
We thank You that You are able!
Amen.

Praying in Time of Need

Be joyful in hope,

patient in affliction,

faithful in prayer.

ROMANS 12:12

We have all heard it said that adversity will either make us bitter or make us better. When a time of adversity came crashing into the lives of Jeff and Kristi, testing their relationship and all they believed, prayer not only saw them through their bitter circumstances, but also made their relationship stronger than they had ever thought possible.

Six months after he was born, Jeff and Kristi's fourth child, Michael, was diagnosed with leukemia. They soon learned from the doctors that the only treatment that could save their tiny son's life was a bone marrow transplant. The news almost crushed them.

What will happen to our child? they wondered. *Who can be a bone marrow donor? How can we bear to see our son suffer? What about the medical bills?* All they knew to do was to seek the help of their gracious Lord.

Almost immediately, their prayers of desperation helped them recognize God's hand at work. Jeff had recently taken a new teaching position. In fact, he had begun his new job the very day Michael was born, and the new assignment had brought their family close to the medical facility where Michael would receive his treatment. When they began a search for a bone marrow donor, they found that their six-year-old daughter, Amy, was a perfect match.

When two people cling to each other in a crisis and pour out their feelings to a God they both trust and love, there is a merging and blending that weaves them together at their deepest levels.

DR. NEAL CLARK WARREN

When the worst happens, the best is yet to be.

CORRIE TEN BOOM

But all their cares were not addressed quite so easily. Their insurance company informed them that there was a one-year waiting period before their new policy would cover the bone marrow transplant. The treatment would cost more than 200,000 dollars—a sum totally out of reach for Jeff and Kristi. Jeff already sold encyclopedias on the side to support their family. Kristi homeschooled their kids. They rented their home. Paying a bill that size was impossible. So they began a round of appeals—to the insurance company and to the highest authority in heaven, knowing well that He who moves the hearts of kings could change the minds of the insurance executives.

The doctors had told them that little Michael's type of leukemia was like a time bomb: It could smolder for twenty-four months or aggressively take over his body in only two weeks. Obviously, the transplant could not wait. Yet the insurance company would not budge from its position and refused to cover the cost.

Michael was hospitalized a dozen times in four months. Each time,

Jeff and Kristi clung to God in prayer. *Please heal Michael!* they cried out to Him.

The couple kept praying. They did not view their prayers as some kind of formula, nor did they see God as some kind of heavenly vending machine. Rather, they learned to invite God into this difficult arena with them and to hold onto His hand for comfort and assurance through all their hours of anguish.

You have seen me tossing and turning through the night. You have collected all my tears and preserved them in your bottle! You have recorded every one in your book.

PSALM 56:8, TLB

Through their brokenhearted prayers for Michael, their hearts were softened toward each other. Often the death or medical crisis of a child can drive a wedge between a couple, but this experience brought Jeff and Kristi closer together. Jeff hurt for his wife and realized the deep sorrow of her heart. Kristi, in turn, felt Jeff's pain. Praying helped them realize how poor in spirit and needy they were.

God answered their prayers in amazing ways—but very differently from what they had imagined. Rather than directly healing Michael or changing the minds of the insurance executives, He began touching the hearts of other people.

Damon, a boy in Jeff's physical education class for students with special needs, emptied his savings account and brought his teacher twelve five-dollar bills. The principal of the school was so touched by the child's generosity that he opened a bank account for Michael. Soon many students and teachers joined in the effort to raise funds for the transplant. Dozens of adults and children raced to help meet the financial needs of Michael's family, making great sacrifices of their time, energy, and money. In less than four weeks more than 227,000 dollars had been raised, and Jeff and Kristi were able to pursue the treatment their son needed to save his life.

But their ordeal was only beginning. Michael faced drastic chemotherapy and radiation treatments even before the bone marrow transplant. As the donor, their little daughter would be in the hospital as well. Prayer was the only way Jeff and Kristi could cope with what they were facing.

Let us pray for the Spirit of prayer. He will take us into the workshop where the power conduits lie. Above the door of this room is written: "Nothing shall be impossible for you."

O. HALLESBY

When Michael was admitted to the hospital for surgery, they again realized how important prayer was to them as a couple.

"Are either of you drinkers?" the hospital's social worker asked them. "It's not unusual for parents of kids undergoing something of this magnitude to have problems in their relationship. Sometimes the stress is so great that parents abandon the whole process—or one spouse abandons the other."

"That's not our method of coping," Jeff replied. Their method of coping was prayer.

While their tiny son was in the hospital, Jeff and Kristi were like ships passing in the night. One was usually at home while the other was at the hospital. Their spirits were woven together by prayer and the mystery of God's grace working within them. For fifty days their baby son was separated from them in a sterilized environment, with no skin-to-skin contact with his mother or father. Jeff and Kristi ached to hold and touch their son and comfort him as he received the harsh, lifesaving treatment.

God's Word became their hope; His compassion their comfort. They knew that every sorrow was accounted for, every tear collected in His bottle, and every prayer recorded in His book. They felt vulnerable and small, but they were just the right size for their Father's lap. And together they rested there.

All of these events happened eight years ago. Their heavenly Father has loaned Michael back to them, cancer free, and he brings delight to his family every day. Even though they would never have chosen for something like this to happen, Jeff and Kristi realize that they serve a Father who knows best and that any circumstances God places them in can be transformed into stepping stones of His grace.

P R A Y E R   E X E R C I S E

In His Hands

Spend some time together holding hands and just sitting before God. In your mind's eye, envision yourself holding *His* hand in whatever circumstances you are facing.

Maybe you picture Jesus as your shepherd, holding you, the sheep. Or maybe you see yourself as a child running into your Father's arms, where sympathy, love, and strength meet every need.

Let your weaknesses or vulnerabilities draw you closer to God and to each other. Bask in the warmth of His love for you and the truth that He promises to be with you forever.

Sunrise Blessing

Are you hurting? Pray.

Do you feel great? Sing.

Are you sick? Call the church leaders together to pray

and anoint you with oil in the name of the Master.

Believing-prayer will heal you,

and Jesus will put you on your feet.

JAMES 5:14–15, THE MESSAGE

One Saturday afternoon as our boys were coming in from playing outside, I heard six-year-old Justin wheezing as he tried to breathe. As usual when I heard that, I darted to the kitchen to get his medicine.

Justin had experienced recurrent asthma attacks from the time he was four. Often he would spend five or more days in the hospital on heavy medication, oxygen, and IVs before his breathing would return to normal.

As our doctor explained it, controlling asthma was like stopping a ball from rolling down a hill—you wanted to catch it before it went very far. Even more than usual, we wanted to head off this attack at the pass. Holmes had scheduled a trip to Dallas for the two of them, and they planned to leave the next morning. Their bags were packed, and Justin couldn't wait to go with his dad. But now this!

A violent round of coughing spurred me to work faster as I gathered up his stuff. We would do the usual things to try to keep the attack under control—have Justin use his inhaler as many times as was safe, give him large amounts of fluid, and administer the medication the doctor prescribed for use only in an acute attack. If all else failed, we'd call the doctor and head to his office or the emergency room. Our usual strategy also included prayer for our son—after we called the doctor.

This time it was different. As Holmes and I were talking about Justin's condition and the special trip they had planned, it suddenly struck us that we had been doing things backwards. The doctor, the prescriptions, and the medical help were all certainly crucial. But why not call on God *first*? After all, He is the Great Physician.

So Holmes and I went over to where Justin lay on the couch and began to pray. We asked the Lord for the asthma attack to not worsen and to give us wisdom so we would know what to do. We petitioned Him to strengthen our son and help him breathe better. As we continued to pray quietly, Justin coughed and coughed. I remember thinking, *Here I am asking God to heal our son. But I don't really know what He says in His Word about it. When does He heal, and how we should approach Him? I*

We cannot create the wind or set it in motion, but we can set our sails to catch it when it comes; we cannot make the electricity, but we can stretch the wire upon which it is to run and do its work. We cannot in a word, control the Spirit, but we can so place ourselves before the Lord, and so do the things He has bidden us do, that we will come under the influence and power of His mighty breath.

THE INDEPENDENT

know that when He was on earth, Jesus healed people with just a touch or a word, but does He still do that today?

Two years before, Holmes and I had begun to read the Bible on a regular basis and had come into a vibrant, daily relationship with God. But we had received very little Bible teaching in our church, no messages from the pulpit on prayer, and nothing about healing.

As my thoughts went back to the Bible, a sudden curiosity replaced the usual anxiety I felt in these situations. What did the Bible say about healing? *Lord, You said if we call on You, You will show us great and mighty things that we do not know* (Jeremiah 33:3). *We don't know anything about this, and we have to find out! Please help us.*

When I told Holmes what I was thinking, he concurred. In fact, some of the same thoughts were running through his mind. So we started searching the house to see if we had any materials or books that might have a chapter on healing and prayer. I checked the shelves in the family room and a cabinet in the garage where we kept books. While I was perusing the bookshelf in our bedroom, my eyes spotted a Bible study that seemed to be exactly what we were looking for. Its title was *What the Bible Says about Healing.* After purchasing it, I had tucked it away without reading it.

Now it looked like the answer to our prayer. Justin's coughing had subsided, and he had fallen asleep, so Holmes and I sat with our Bibles at the kitchen table and began to look up the study's recommended Scriptures: Isaiah 53:5; Psalm 30:2; Jeremiah 17:4; Matthew 4:23; and others. As we read the verses, we talked about them and prayed together as they seemed to direct.

With each verse, my heart leaped with hope. God *does* still heal people today—spiritually, emotionally, and physically. In fact, one of His names is *Jehovah Rapha,* the Lord our Healer (Exodus 15:26). We found specific verses to pray in times of sickness. And the more we read in God's Word, the more we realized that He *does* care about our son's condition and that His power could be released through prayer.

We continued to work on the study through the evening while Chris and Alison, our two younger children, ate their dinner and played beside us in the kitchen. Later, after we'd read the kids a story and tucked them in their beds, Holmes and I filled our coffee cups and returned to our Bibles to complete the study. Justin was again wheezing and breathing rapidly, but when we gave him his nighttime medicine, he settled back down and was able to get some rest.

I had always been the first to run to the doctor, and I was vigilant about doing everything he said; but this time, I somehow had the confidence not to dash to the emergency room or make a panicked call to the asthma specialist. There was something in God's Word, some piece of the puzzle that we still needed, something God wanted to teach us.

About three o'clock in the morning, we read one of the last verses in the study from a passage in James 5. The verse said that when someone was sick, Christians were to call the church elders to pray over him and anoint him with oil in the Lord's name. We had never noticed that verse before. Elders praying for the sick? Oil? The church we attended didn't do that. It sounded unusual, but God's Word seemed to point clearly to this prescription.

Our motivation increased when we read what the Bible said next: "And the prayer of faith will save him who is sick, and the Lord will restore him" (James 5:15, AMP). What a promise!

But where could we find someone to do this?

"We need to have some elders—somebody who believes this—come pray for Justin," I told Holmes. As we pondered that, I remembered two young pastors from another local church we had visited recently. Granted, they weren't elders at our church, but they were the leaders of their church.

"Steve and Jeff! I bet they pray for sick people," I said. "Why don't we call them right now?"

"I don't know," Holmes replied cautiously. "It's the middle of the night. We'd be waking them up."

"But this is close to being an emergency," I replied. "Surely if doctors get up in the middle of the night, elders would too. Let me see if I can find a phone number."

A few minutes later I got Steve on the phone and told him the situation. He groggily but patiently listened as I told him about Justin's asthma attack and what we'd learned from the Bible.

I asked, "Would you and Jeff come and pray for our son like it says here in James? It says to call for the elders to pray.... It's the one thing that's never been done for him, and we know it would make a difference."

"I tell you what," Steve proposed, "I'll start praying now, and you all try to get some sleep. We'll be over there in a little while."

Holmes and I were so excited that we couldn't sleep. Instead, we stayed up the rest of the night, intermittently praying, reading the Bible, taking care of Justin, and waiting for the elders to arrive. My anticipation matched that of a child on Christmas Eve.

At 5:30 A.M. we heard a quiet knock on the door, and there stood Jeff and Steve with guitar, Bible, and a little vial of oil. We thanked them for coming and chatted in the kitchen for a few minutes. Then they went

God joyfully employs an infinite variety of means to bring health and well-being to his people. We are glad for God's friends, the doctors, who with skill and compassion help our bodies fight against disease and sickness.... We also celebrate the growing army of women and men and children who are learning how to bring the healing power of Christ to others for the glory of God and the good of all concerned.

RICHARD FOSTER

into the family room where Justin was resting on the couch.

"Justin, we'd like to pray for you and ask God to make you well. Would that be okay?" Jeff asked.

"Sure."

"We're going to touch your forehead here with a little oil, just like the Bible says," Jeff said as he read the verses in James. As the two men began to pray, nothing happened immediately. But a sense of peace permeated the space all around us.

As they continued, Justin relaxed and became very still. Then suddenly he called, "Mom, I think I'm going to throw up!" and I ran for a pan. In a few minutes the thick mucus that had been plugging his bronchial tubes came up—the very thing that happens when he is given adrenalin shots in the emergency room. Only this time it wasn't a painful round of injections causing an adrenalin rush—it was God's power.

The angels of God are much nearer in our seasons of prayer than we imagine. God employs these glorious heavenly intelligences in the blessed work of hearing and answering prayer.

E. M. BOUNDS

Justin's breathing began to slow down, and the wheezing gradually subsided. In just a short time, he sat up, and a few minutes later a rosy color came back into his cheeks. Steve began to play his guitar, and we all sang "Great is the Lord" and "Jesus, Name above All Names."

The early morning light began to gleam through the windows as Jeff strummed the guitar and we quietly sang, "This is the day, this is the day that the Lord has made, I will rejoice...." God's presence filled the room and our hearts. I looked over at our son. His blue eyes were shining brightly, and his cheeks were flushed as if he'd just come in from playing G.I. Joe in the park instead of struggling all night with an asthma attack. A grin spread over his face as he said, "Dad, are we still leaving this morning for our trip? I packed yesterday!"

As the men were leaving, Justin, his eyes wide open in wonder, asked me, "Did you see that, Mom? Did you see the angel standing beside me when Jeff and Steve were praying? It was very bright and shiny, all white and glowing. You must have seen it!" Holmes and I hadn't seen anything but sunlight streaming in the windows and our son, who had been sick but now was well. But that was enough to show us God's amazing power and love.

Later that morning, Holmes and Justin waved to us as they drove out of the driveway—just as they had planned. They had a marvelous adventure together in Texas. After they left, I dressed Chris and Alison in their Sunday best, and we headed for church. When we sang the hymns that morning, there was a new song in my heart and a fountain of thanksgiving as I joined the congregation in praising God, our almighty, glorious Savior and wonderful Healer.

Prayer Exercise

A Prayer for Healing

Study God's Word and ask His Spirit to teach you how to pray effectively for those around you who are suffering. And next time you or someone in your family is ill, even as you utilize the doctors and medicines that God has provided, don't hesitate to call on Him and upon the leaders of your church to pray as James 5 suggests.

A Prayer of Thanks

Always keep on praying.

No matter what happens, always be thankful,

for this is God's will for you

who belong to Christ Jesus.

1 THESSALONIANS 5:17–18, NLT

t was snowing again. Really snowing. The snow and ice pil-
ing up around their chalet high in the Austrian Alps had
already held Dave and Claudia Arp captive for most of their
Christmas vacation in 1999.

Austria had once been their home and ministry base, so they had
looked forward to spending some time where they had once lived. When
they first arrived, Claudia had a cold and couldn't ski. By the time she
was well, the ice had built up on the mountain, and the weather wasn't
good for skiing. They really couldn't get out much either. They had a
rental car, but since it had summer tires, they were afraid it would get
stuck in the snow or, worse, slide off the ice-packed roads. Although
they had come to relax, not sightsee, they were frustrated at not being
able to drive around on the mountain roads. To add to that, their cell
phone modem wouldn't work, so they were cut off from e-mail from
friends back in the States.

For two weeks, Dave and Claudia had stayed inside by the open fire.

They slept, wrote Christmas cards, and very carefully took long walks in the ice-packed snow. But it was getting old. *What a bummer!* they thought. They'd been going to Austria in the winter for years, and this had never happened.

Both explorers, they loved to drive and find picturesque places to hike. But they couldn't even drive to their favorite restaurant on top of Pass Thun or visit the church in nearby Mittersill, where their son had been married a decade ago. Their pleasant time of R & R was turning to sheer boredom.

Happy are the couples who do recognize that their happiness is a gift of God, who can kneel to express their thanks not only for the love which he has put in their hearts, the children he has given them, or all of life's joys, but also for the progress in their marriage which he brings about through that hard school of mutual understanding.

PAUL TOURNIER

God had slowed them down.

Now, on this last evening of Dave and Claudia's getaway, it started to snow again. They slipped out of their chalet and walked for an hour in the fresh snow. Each step left a clean, deep footprint. The white snow illuminated the night sky and brightened the darkness of the surrounding landscape. They could see the peaceful village below, the farms on the rolling hills, and even the majestic Tyrolean Alps towering above them.

Previously, walking had been difficult because of the ice, but with the new snow, walking became effortless. Each step was secure. No slipping or falling. Everything glowed with beauty. As if just for them, God had painted their world a beautiful, gentle white. No gaudy colored Christmas tree lights or Santas climbing chimneys. No commercials shouting "Buy me!" No ringing phones, e-mails, or faxes to answer.

As Dave and Claudia reveled in their walk, they both sensed God whisper, "I brought you here to renew you—body and soul. And just as you are glorying in this walk in the new snow, I want you to walk, a year older and a year wiser, into the new millennium. I have called you to make a path for others to follow. Walk toward the Light, and I will be with you every step of the way."

As the gentle snowflakes continued to fall, Dave and Claudia paused and lifted their hearts to the Lord. *Thank You, Lord, for the freshly fallen snow and for renewing our bodies and our souls. Thank You for fresh hope and vision for this new millennium we are entering. Thank You that Your light will make a clear path for us and for others to follow. Thank You for letting us be a small part of all the positive things that are happening because of You!*

It was a simple prayer of thanksgiving. No requests—only praise. But that prayer in the snow is still having a profound impact on their lives as Dave and Claudia seek to follow God's path.

Today, as the daffodils send forth their brilliant yellow blooms and tender green leaves appear once again on the trees, they are reminded of the majesty of our God, the giver of life. They remember that God is their encourager. As they race through airports to speaking engagements and ministry assignments, as they labor to meet deadlines and deal with daily correspondence and demands on their time, they are reminded that He is walking with them today—just as He did on that snow-covered path in the Alps.[4]

Isn't it time to stop and simply say, "Thank You"?

Worship is the "thank you" that refuses to be silenced.

M A X   L U C A D O

Thanksgiving nourishes the prayer life and opens the channel for richer blessings.

A N O N Y M O U S

PRAYER EXERCISE

SAYING THANK YOU TO GOD

Take time to express your thanks to God together. You may not be able to do it on a walk in the Alps as this couple did, but you could stroll to somewhere beautiful in your area or sit in your backyard after dark and look around at all that God has created. Remember aloud the things He has done for you in the past. Think about how He is sustaining you even now in the midst of your circumstances. Be refreshed as you "enter his gates with thanksgiving and his courts with praise" (Psalm 100:4).

Can we expect future mercies,

if we are not thankful for past blessings?

WILLIAM W. PATTON

A Prayer of Thanksgiving

Lord, so often we are asking You for things.
You told us to ask, seek, and knock—
but You also tell us to always be thankful
and to pray with thanksgiving. That's where we often fall down.
So often we are talking to You about what You haven't done yet
and about what we want You to do instead of thanking You
for what You have already done for us!
So we take this time to praise You for who You are—
the Mighty God, the Everlasting God, Lord of lords,
God of all comfort, our refuge and hope.
Thank You for our family, our home, and our church.
Thank You for the love You have put in our hearts.
We give thanks for all the joys we've experienced
and the many ways You have provided in the past.
And we even thank You for the problems we're currently dealing with
because they draw us closer to You
and give us one more opportunity to seek You.
Thank You for this season of life and for the gift of today—
another day to love and learn and grow together.
Most of all, thank You for the gift of Your son, Jesus,
so we can know You and have hope for today and for eternity.
Amen.

Finding God's Will

If you want favor with both God and man,

and a reputation for good judgment and common sense,

then trust the Lord completely.... In everything you do, put God first,

and he will direct you and crown your efforts with success.

PROVERBS 3:4–6, TLB

Lord, help us to make the right decision. Show us Your will and guide us, Ken Cooper and his wife, Millie, prayed fervently. They had a tough decision to make: whether to accept the promotion the Air Force was offering or to move to Dallas to establish the first-of-its-kind aerobics center that Cooper had envisioned. The choice they made would dramatically impact their lives.

No one had even heard of aerobics until Dr. Ken Cooper's landmark book, *Aerobics,* was published in 1968 and made the *New York Times* bestseller list. Ken had spent several years in the Army and more than ten years as an Air Force physician. During that time, he designed an aerobics program to condition astronauts for space travel, and he subsequently tested it on more than twenty-seven thousand people on military bases around the country.

With only seven years to retirement, Ken was a lieutenant colonel stationed in San Antonio. The U.S. had paid for his graduate studies at Harvard in public health and exercise physiology, and he had served the time needed to pay back the public. In six more months he would become a full colonel. But at the same time, the Air Force had backed out of the space program, and NASA had taken over. His new orders: Move out of research and to a hospital command—an administrative post.

We are to pray in times of adversity, lest we become faithless and unbelieving. We are to pray in times of prosperity, lest we become boastful and proud. We need to pray in times of security, less we become self-sufficient.

BILLY GRAHAM

The Coopers carefully considered each option. Ken was almost forty years old. They had a five-year-old daughter, and Millie was pregnant with their second child. If he left the Air Force, they would have no severance pay, no health insurance, only twenty-five thousand dollars in savings, and no wealthy relatives to help them. It would be risky to move to Dallas where Ken was an unknown. What's more, the chances of success looked like one in a million. Nevertheless, Ken wanted to prove that it was "easier and more effective to maintain good health than it was to regain it once it was lost."

Ken and Millie sought the counsel of trusted friends, pastors, and businessmen. Many people advised them against a move to Dallas. "You have only seven years left until retirement and a nice income for the rest of your life…it would be foolish to move! Stay in the Air Force!" Still unsure, they decided to step up their prayers for wisdom. For three days and nights the Coopers prayed, consciously entrusting their lives to the Holy Spirit's control and asking God to show them His will. While they prayed, they sensed God's direction to go to Dallas.

So in 1970, the Coopers turned down the Air Force's lucrative offer and moved to Dallas. From a tiny office in a strip mall shopping center, they squeezed by on book royalties and borrowed money as they looked for land for the center and awaited the birth of their second child.

Almost immediately, they ran into a huge obstacle. Because Ken wasn't a cardiologist, the physicians' Board of Censors questioned his practices—especially his use of the treadmill for stress tests—and called him to appear before them. It was a critical moment—the board had the power to stop Cooper from practicing medicine and to block his plans for the aerobics center. Ken and Millie surrounded the meeting with prayer, and Ken remembers feeling God's special presence with him as he explained his philosophy of preventive medicine to the Board of Censors. Eventually, he was allowed to proceed.

God has new developments and new resources. He can do new things, unheard-of things, hidden things. Let us enlarge our hearts and not limit Him.

ANDREW MURRAY

During this time, Millie grew so apprehensive that she developed a severe case of dermatitis. Cooper reassured her, telling her not to worry about anything—except for getting their baby here! But he understood her fears. He, too, feared that he wouldn't make it financially, that they might have to abandon his dream and return to the Air Force or open a general practice to provide for the family. But as they continued to pray, and as they faced each obstacle and task, they began to see God work in amazing ways.

Driving around with his real estate agent, Ken saw a piece of property that would be perfect for his dream: twenty-two acres with two lakes and beautiful trees.

"It's impossible to get this land rezoned. The neighbors are solid in their resistance," the agent told him. But Ken insisted on talking to the owner about selling him 8.6 acres. The first time he and his agent talked to Mrs. Clarice Nichols, the widow who owned the land, she gave them a firm no. She absolutely would not sell 8.6 acres of her land for Cooper's aerobics center.

The Coopers kept on praying for God's will and for the land he needed.

A few weeks later the agent talked with Mrs. Nichols a second time. Suddenly her eyes lit up. "Is this the doctor who wrote the book on exercise?" She remembered that she had heard Cooper's inspirational message in Colorado Springs the year before. She changed her mind about selling Cooper some land.

We do not pray to get things from God, but as we pray God changes us until His will becomes our will.

RUTH BELL GRAHAM

Then another obstacle arose—finding a bank to loan him the purchase price of 1.2 million dollars. Ken had no significant assets, and bank after bank turned him down. Finally, Joe McKinney, the president of a local corporation who had read Ken's book, offered him an interest-free loan.

As the Aerobics Center grew, other challenges kept the Coopers on their knees before God. One pivotal situation developed when their bank, one of the largest in the state, failed in the late 1980s, and an out-of-state bank took over their loan. Although the Coopers had never missed a payment, the new bank called their note—a situation that threatened to close the center's doors and push them into bankruptcy. Again, Ken turned everything over to God. The property wasn't his, he acknowledged—it was God's, and he was only the custodian. God would do with it what He wanted; Cooper's job was to be the best custodian he could be.

Three difficult years of legal and financial battles followed, but the Aerobics Center stayed open. In time, it began to flourish. Today, the Aerobics Center has grown to include seven divisions occupying thirty acres. It has 450 employees and has recently launched Dr. Cooper's program, "Healthy Living 2000," which is broadcast both on the radio and the Internet. Every day he helps people assess, manage, and improve their personal health and fitness.

And it all started when a husband and wife sought God's will together in prayer, and then moved ahead in faith.

PRAYER EXERCISE

SEEKING GOD'S WILL

If you are facing a decision, seek godly counsel, ask God for His Holy Spirit's leading, and study His Word. Most importantly, pray together as a couple—diligently, as Ken and Millie Cooper prayed—in the faith that God will direct your steps.

God's power in us who believe, is great beyond measure…
So! When He comes in and starts business,
we are likely to be surprised by any kind of miracle!
Diseases may vanish with our prayers.
Mountains may be moved. The world may applaud.
One has every reason to stand on tiptoe with expectancy.
For God loves surprises, and He can do anything.
The motto is right which says:
"Expect great things from God. Attempt great things for God."

FRANK LAUBACH

Back in Business

"I also tell you this—if two of you agree

down here on earth concerning anything you ask for,

my Father in heaven will do it for you."

MATTHEW 18:19, TLB

Our children had just left for school when Holmes and I felt compelled to kneel by our bed and seek God. After reading aloud part of Psalm 37, we petitioned the Lord for a building project that would restart Holmes's business. We didn't just say a quick, *Hey, God, bless our family and bless Holmes's work.* We were earnest, unified, and in agreement about our exact need and what we were asking God to do.

We had been back in Oklahoma almost a year with no construction work for Holmes. We had returned because he had the prospect of building a custom home for a family but, upon our arrival, we learned that the couple didn't have the money to begin. They had planned to finance their dream home from an inheritance—but their elderly relative had not yet died!

Holmes found temporary work in a clothing store but became increasingly frustrated with sorting shirts. More than once we found ourselves counting change on the dining-room table before heading for the grocery store.

The answers to all our problems can be had through contact with Almighty God.

BILLY GRAHAM

Sometimes we are afraid that we do not have enough faith to pray for this child or that marriage. Our fears should be put to rest, for the Bible tells us great miracles are possible through faith the size of a tiny mustard seed.

RICHARD FOSTER

We were desperate! Holding hands, we prayed to God with all our hearts, *Lord, send work! Soon! If You want Holmes to be in the building business, we ask You to open doors for him. Please restore Holmes's building business and bring an opportunity,* I added.

I don't know how much time elapsed, but we prayed up a storm that morning, and as we got up from our moments together in God's presence, we had a peaceful sense that heaven had heard. Holmes grabbed his brown-bag lunch and left for the clothing store. I put breakfast dishes in the dishwasher and threw a load of clothes in the washer before sitting down to my computer to write a magazine article.

Within the hour, the phone's shrill ring interrupted my thoughts.

"Is this Holmes Fuller's office?" a lady on the other end of the line asked.

I assured her that it was. (Holmes and I shared an office. He used it in the evenings.)

The woman went on: "Years ago when we lived here in the city, my husband and I saw several of the wonderful homes he had built, and we were very impressed. So I'm wondering, is Holmes still in the building business?"

Before I could answer, the woman said, "I always wanted a Holmes Fuller house. But my husband was transferred, and we moved to the East Coast. When we moved back here after a few years, we had to buy a house rather quickly and didn't have time to build one. We've never really liked this one, so we've decided to sell it and build our own. I've talked to several builders and, in fact, had settled on one who was ready to sign a contract to build our home.

"But just this morning the strangest thing happened: Holmes Fuller's name kept coming to my mind, and I distinctly remembered those beautiful houses he built. I just thought I'd look in the phone book to see if he was still in the city and if he might be interested in talking with us and seeing our preliminary plans."

Wherever you can agree that touches anything God wants you to accomplish in this life, you have tremendous potential in prayer. You have Jesus' promise that God will hear those prayers and that Jesus will be in your midst whenever you unite in prayer.

BILL AND LYNDI
MCCARTNEY

Would he! I had to restrain myself from leaping to my feet and shouting into the phone. From that one phone call, scarcely an hour after Holmes and I had prayed together, an amazing door of provision swung open.

We rejoiced as we saw God work. Ordinarily it takes months to get a house plan designed and financing approved before breaking ground. But in record time the design was completed, the loan went through, and the house in Apple Valley was begun. Holmes was back in business. From start to finish it was a uniquely blessed project.

PRAYER EXERCISE
OPENED AND CLOSED DOORS

The book of Revelation says that God holds the keys and has the authority to open and close doors. We can trust Him to do both in our lives. Are you and your spouse burdened by an unresolved financial problem or job frustration? Pray together and lift your needs and desires to the Lord. Ask Him to open the doors that would fulfill His plan for you and to close those doors that need to be closed.

You can't believe the changes that will occur in your life—

in your marriage, your family, your career, your ministry...

once you are convinced in the core of your being that God is willing,

that he is able and that he has invited you to come before his throne

and do business in prayer.

BILL HYBELS

A Light in Russia

"Be strong and of good courage; do not be afraid, nor be dismayed,

for the LORD your God is with you wherever you go."

JOSHUA 1:9, NKJV

iana and Oleg knelt beside their bed in their Moscow flat and earnestly prayed that God would give them direction in a decision that would impact their entire lives—whether Oleg should stay in the Russian military. This was no small decision for the Christian couple. This wasn't the first time they had prayed about it, and it wouldn't be the last.

Even with the end of glasnost in the early 1990s, the spiritual climate in the former Soviet Union was one of chilly suspicion and antagonism toward Christians. As a by-product of decades of atheism and communism, many people still associated Christianity with mental illness. Nowhere was this attitude more prevalent than in the Russian army.

After nearly twenty years in the Russian military, Oleg Kondratyev exemplified the career soldier. Born in Gorky City, he attended military school in Leningrad and later a military academy. Life was good for Oleg, his wife, Diana, and their two sons—as good as could be expected in a society with a failing economy and a faltering government.

Diana, an office worker, had accepted Jesus Christ as her personal Savior in 1992 and had begun to pray passionately for her husband. At that time they were very distant from each other emotionally—together, but not very happy. Diana prayed and prayed and prayed some more, but Oleg remained resistant to God and uninterested in the faith his wife had found.

Pray until what you pray for has been accomplished or until you have complete assurance in your heart that it will be.

THE PRACTICE OF PRAYER

The first chink in his armor appeared when the couple visited Diana's parents, and Oleg had a chance to observe their lives. He couldn't avoid asking himself questions like, "Why do they connect their lives with God?" and most of all, "Who is God?"

These questions sparked Oleg to begin reading the Bible, where he learned the truth of God's existence and His love for him. Even so, he resisted a personal commitment to God, considering Him useful only in helping him become more successful. He wanted God's blessings without giving God his heart. Time passed and Diana continued to pray.

Gradually Oleg's inner struggle reached its climax. He believed 1 Corinthians 15:19—"If only for this life we have hope in Christ, we are to be pitied more than all men"—but it took a car wreck to convince Oleg that he had to make a choice: either live with Jesus or die without Him.

In the midst of the wreck, God seemed to say to him, "You know Me, yet do not believe Me. You see My blessings, yet do not love Me." In that moment Oleg made a deliberate choice. He resolved that God was *his* God. He resolved to believe that God truly loved him and that Jesus Christ would be his Lord and Savior forever.

On January 7, 1994, Russia celebrated its independence. That same day Oleg celebrated his own freedom from sin and resolved to live for Christ. He and Diana immediately began setting aside time every night to pray together. They committed to pray in unity about every important decision in their lives. Through their mutual commitment to Jesus Christ and their evening prayer times together, their marriage was renewed.

Oleg's decision for Christ had a positive effect on his marriage, but it posed a huge question for his military career. Should he leave the army? They were willing to do whatever the Lord wanted. Isaiah 6:8 was the cry of their hearts: "Then I heard the voice of the Lord saying, 'Whom shall I send? And who will go for us?' And I said, 'Here am I. Send me!'"

Meanwhile, as news of Oleg's conversion spread, the first to react was his superior officer. Every step Oleg took came under the deepest scrutiny. His chief even told Oleg that he didn't want him in his department. The couple was worried, but they had hope in God and in the power of prayer. They faced many challenges and uncertainties, but this was the biggest of them all.

Oleg and Diana decided to fast and pray for God's will to be clearly revealed. They made a mutual commitment to love and serve Him with all their strength. They claimed God's promise from Joshua 1:9—that as they were strong and of good courage and not afraid, the Lord their God would be with them wherever they went.

Days turned into weeks and weeks into a month before God answered with a miraculous display of His sovereign will: Oleg was promoted to the

Prayer blesses all things, brings all things, relieves all things, and prevents all things. Everything as well as every place and every hour is to be ordered by prayer. Prayer has in it the possibility to affect everything which affects us.

E . M . BOUNDS

rank of colonel, leaving his former superior officer stunned.

At the same time, a group of Christians formed the Moscow Society of Christians in the Military, or Shield of Faith. This group of Christian military personnel, both active and discharged, is committed to bringing the gospel to the Russian Army and shining God's light throughout their country. They elected Oleg president.

Diana is hard at work spreading the ministry of Moms In Touch International throughout the former Soviet Union. Having seen the power of prayer in her life and in the life of her family, she is establishing Moms In Prayer groups throughout Russia. Diana is convinced that mothers' prayers for their children and grandchildren will bring spiritual blessings throughout the land.

God's promises are given not to restrain, but to incite to prayer. They show the direction in which we may ask.... Though the Bible be crowded with golden promises from board to board, yet will they be inoperative until we turn them into prayer.

F. B. MEYER

Oleg and Diana now realize that God's plan for their lives had originated many years earlier—back before Christian churches were once again allowed to meet in Russia. God had put them in the very place He wanted them so that they could share the good news of Jesus Christ, influence the lives of Oleg's commanding officers, and help others learn the blessing of prayer.

As Oleg and Diana shine a light in their country, their lives are living proof that nothing is impossible with God.

PRAYER EXERCISE
COMBINING FASTING AND PRAYER

Throughout the Bible and history, believers have fasted from food in order to focus better on seeking God's will and His kingdom. When Oleg and Diana devoted the time they would normally spend eating to prayer, reading Scripture, and seeking God, He provided clear guidance and confirmation.

When you are facing a decision—where to send your kids to school, whether you should begin a business, or whatever the situation—decide on a period of time and fast as a couple. Ask God to give you a scriptural promise to stand on for your specific need. Then watch and see what He does on your behalf.

A Prayer for Direction

Father of life, You never change.
But circumstances cause us to face many changes
and make countless decisions,
and we're facing one at this time. We need Your guidance today, Lord.
We ask You to fill us with the knowledge of Your will
through all spiritual wisdom and revelation.
We pray this so that we may live a life that pleases You in every way,
bear fruit in every good work, and grow in our knowledge of You.
Enable us to hear Your voice, the voice of our Good Shepherd.
Give us courage to follow the light
You shed on our path, one step at a time,
not with timidity or fear, but with confidence that You are leading
the way and that You have a future and a hope for us.
Amen.

Changing Our World through Prayer

The effective, fervent prayer of a righteous man avails much.

JAMES 5:16, NKJV

ernie and Elaine had been Christians for years. They loved to study the Bible, often taught Sunday school classes, and were always willing to serve in the church. But they had never been much interested in prayer meetings. Oh, they prayed before meals and before bed, and they prayed for their own needs and those of others; but joining a group *just to pray* was not high on their list of priorities.

All that changed when their son began to struggle in school due to a hearing disability. Concern for him brought Elaine to her knees and led her to join a Moms In Touch prayer group. Moms In Touch International (MITI) is an organization that encourages mothers to gather to pray for their children, teachers, and schools.

As Elaine met with others to pray, God began to help her deal with her fears and increase her faith. Long before he saw any changes in their son, Bernie began to see a change in his wife. Once a champion worrier, she suddenly seemed at peace.

One night as they were relaxing in their Jacuzzi, Bernie commented on the changes he saw in Elaine and asked her what they did at the MITI prayer meetings. After Elaine filled him in, he said, "I don't know how you do it—pray for an entire hour—but would you teach me?"

She suggested that they pray right there and then led him through the steps of prayer she had learned at the Moms In Touch meetings: praise, confession, thanksgiving, and intercession. More than an hour later, Bernie and Elaine emerged from the Jacuzzi, laughing at their prunelike appearance and excited about their time in prayer. They had no idea that God had just laid the foundation for a radical change in the direction of their lives.

In the days and weeks that followed, God taught Bernie and Elaine more and more about His heart for prayer. Bernie began to get up earlier in the mornings in order to have an extra hour to pray before he did his Bible study. And as God reminded them to pray throughout the day, they both began to understand the concept of "praying without ceasing." Bernie and Elaine became especially impressed with the importance of praise, repentance, and thanksgiving in their times of talking to God. They discovered that as they praised God for His character, they displayed more of His character in their lives. They also saw that as they surrendered their sin and self-will to God in repentance, God gave them power and victory despite their weaknesses. And the more they gave thanks for what He had done, the more aware they became of His work all around them.

> *God could have shown up at any time, but over and over in the Bible, He revealed Himself when people began to pray.*
>
> JIM CYMBALA

They learned more about prayer from prayer warriors such as Dick Eastman and Joy Dawson. One lesson that stood out in particular was on the importance of waiting on God in silence as they prayed. This felt rather unnatural at first, and it took a deliberate effort on their part to learn to quiet themselves and wait before the Lord. But the results were well worth it. During these times, God often spoke to their hearts and directed their prayers in ways they would not have thought of on their own. They discovered that in times of surrendered silence, God brought them into agreement with His mind and will, and as a result, their prayers were much more effective. Sometimes they heard nothing in these times; they simply thanked God for the privilege of waiting before His throne.

Prayer has power because it brings believing souls into oneness with the operation of God the Father, the Son, and the Holy Spirit. Prayer is therefore a partnership and cooperation with the Trinity. How very essential is our part in that partnership and cooperation!

ANDREW MURRAY

As Bernie and Elaine's prayer lives grew, the focus of their prayers changed. God had initially brought them to prayer through concern for *their* son. But as they spent time in prayer, He gave them the concerns of His Son. God also increased their love for the lost in their community and gave them a burden for reconciliation and unity in the church.

God began to unite Bernie and Elaine with others who were feeling the same way, and together they started a prayer group to pray for the pastors, churches, and lost people of their community. Each time they met, they spent time in praise and confession and then, before anyone uttered a prayer request, quietly waited. Five, ten, or fifteen minutes later, when they did begin to intercede, they would be amazed at how God had directed two or more of them to pray in exactly the same way.

Although the participants in the prayer group came from a variety of churches and denominational backgrounds, they repeatedly experienced one accord in their prayers. Bernie and Elaine have come to believe that this kind of agreement is what Jesus refers to in Matthew 18:19–20: "If two of you on earth agree about anything you ask for, it will be done for you by my Father in heaven. For where two or three come together in my name, there am I with them." They knew that this verse doesn't promise that when two people agree on a man-centered idea, God will perform it. Rather, when two or more people sense God's leading and then pray aloud and discover they are in agreement, they have an assurance that "it will be done."

People who make opportunity for the Holy Spirit to speak to them know that the Christian life is a continual adventure. It is full of surprises, thrills, challenges and mysteries.

BILL HYBELS

When Bernie, Elaine, and their friends started praying together for their local churches to unite and reach out to the lost, few of the pastors in the city even knew one another. To the best of anyone's knowledge, there had never been a community-wide prayer meeting. Now, four years later, more than twenty of the community's pastors pray together monthly. For the past two years, the pastors have also sponsored a multidenominational prayer gathering on the National Day of Prayer. The first year, three hundred people attended this gathering. The second year, more than six hundred attended. This year's assembly will be held at the largest church in town in anticipation of an even greater crowd.

Bernie and Elaine can hardly believe all they have seen God do since that night long ago in their Jacuzzi. They are quick to add that all of their prayers, and those of the prayer group, add up to only a drop in the oceans of prayer that have gone into what is happening in their community. But they have come to realize that the most important thing they can do, whether in dealing with personal needs or with worldwide concerns, is to cry out to God in prayer. It may be that He will lead them to do things they had not anticipated, and they are truly excited about what God has in store for the future.

We are not ready for the battle until we have seen the Lord,

for Jesus is the answer to all problems.

CORRIE TEN BOOM

Prayer Exercise
The Four Steps of Prayer

Use the four steps of prayer outlined here to guide your prayer time as a couple.

Praise—Focus on God by reading about His attributes and character in Psalms and reflecting those verses back to Him in prayer.

Confession—Psalm 66:18 says, "If I regard iniquity in my heart, the Lord will not hear me" (AMP). Confession can be silent or spoken. Ask God to reveal your sins so you can confess them to Him and have a clean heart.

Thanksgiving—Thank God for His forgiveness (1 John 1:9) and for all the ways He has blessed you or answered your prayers.

Intercession—Pray for each other, for your children, and for others whom God places on your heart.

Before you come to God in intercession, ask Him to crucify your own logic, thoughts, and desires, and to set apart your mind to hear only Him. This will enable you to pray according to His will and desires rather than your own. Then wait quietly. Don't be afraid of silence. Silence before God is valuable. It is not a waste of time! Sometimes God speaks to us clearly as we wait before Him, and sometimes there is only silence.

When you don't get a strong leading to pray, you can still tell God that He is worthy and that you are honored to sit before His throne. Maintain the attitude, "If You say something, Lord, we're thrilled. But even if You don't, it's a privilege to sit in Your presence!"

The Ripple Effect

As the rain and snow come down from heaven

and stay upon the ground to water the earth,

and cause the grain to grow and to produce seed for the farmer

and bread for the hungry, so also is my Word.

I send it out and it always produces fruit.

It shall accomplish all I want it to, and prosper everywhere I send it.

ISAIAH 55:10–11, TLB

When Scott and Evelyn's firstborn son, Lucas, went away to college, it was tough for them. Lucas's senior year of high school had been fantastic. He had been one of the top-rated runners in the state of Florida and a role model for his classmates—captain of his track and cross-country team and president of the Fellowship of Christian Athletes. Lucas was the pride and joy of his father's heart, and he and his dad were buds, *good* buds. Now he would be attending a university five hundred miles from home.

As Scott and Evelyn drove away from the college campus, watching Lucas get smaller and smaller in the rearview window, their hearts ached. They knew that God was going to take care of their son. They remembered when Lucas had become a Christian: Scott had led his son to the Lord when Lucas was in ninth grade—right there in the family garage. Lucas had a solid spiritual foundation, so they weren't worried about that.

Prayer is not just icing on the cake of a so-called spiritual life; prayer is warm, close communication with the living God and also a matter of doing an active work on His side of the battle.

EDITH SCHAEFFER

Our prayers are God's opportunities.

FREDERICK WILLIAM

FARRAR

But Lucas was attending college on a track scholarship and would still be competing. Scott and Evelyn would miss being there to cheer him on as they had during his high school years. They also knew that Lucas would never again be at home to stay; he would only come home to visit. Although they had raised Lucas to become independent, nobody had told them how painful it would be for them when he struck out on his own. Missing their son already, they prayed for him all the way home.

As Evelyn and he continued to pray for their son, Scott felt a strong nudge to get connected on the Internet. The Internet had never been a part of Scott's daily life; in fact, he'd personally seen no use for it. But now he decided that he would learn to use e-mail, even though it was a struggle for him.

With newfound skills and an e-mail address, Scott started writing to Lucas every day. When Lucas was in high school, they had had daily devotionals together, so it was natural for Scott to continue sharing devotional thoughts via the Net. Scott also sent Lucas a Scripture verse and then "prayed with" him at the end of each message. Writing daily "e-devotionals" helped Scott adjust to Lucas's absence.

Scott was able to attend a track meet or two and meet some of the guys on the university team. They had seen several of the daily devotionals he had sent his son, and they asked if they could receive them too. So Scott began writing Lucas's friends as well. Often they wrote back, asking his advice about a relationship or some other challenge they were facing. Soon, what had begun as therapy for a lonesome dad grew into a bona fide ministry.

As Scott continued to write, he and Evelyn prayed daily that God would use these devotionals to keep His hand on their son's life as well as direct and guide the lives of the other young people who read them.

More things are wrought by prayer
Than this world dreams of.

ALFRED LORD
TENNYSON

One day, while midway through a series he was writing on stewardship, Scott felt bogged down. His thoughts simply weren't coming together. That evening he and Evelyn prayed together for guidance, clarity, and for the Lord's will to be done.

As the Lord has made every leaf different, so also He shows limitless variety and divine ingenuity in answering prayer.

CAMERON V. THOMPSON

At 4:00 A.M. the next morning, the time he normally wrote and e-mailed the devotions, Scott was still dreading writing the lesson. He also felt guilty that he had made so little progress on it. So he checked his incoming mail first and found this message from a student at the University of North Florida:

Mr. McCurdy:

I've been meaning to write you for some time now. Your e-mail devotions have been a great encouragement to me. I've been so worried recently about my grades and my future and things. Your words have made me realize that I don't need to dwell on those worries. I mean, sure, I'm doing my best in my classes and training hard, but I need to relax from the worrying and realize that God is in control of all things. Sometimes it's hard when all I am surrounded with is the daily routine of the world.

Thank you for making me stop and think about how things really are. Sometimes the best part of my day is when I read your devotions.

Thank you very much,

Caleb

Scott cried when he read that e-mail. He went to find Evelyn. "You know, I'm so vain. For some reason I thought these devotions were about *me* and how they sounded. They are not about me, or how I feel about them! These devotions are God's words that will touch the lives of these young people, and as they're sent out, God will accomplish what He plans for them to do. I'm just the tool; He is the craftsman."

With that realization, Scott's whole thought pattern changed. God was faithful to show him just what to write that morning—and for many mornings afterward.

Scott's e-mail list now includes hundreds of college students in eight universities around the country. His e-devotionals cover such topics as relationships, marriage, money, possessions, stewardship, and career guidance. He also sends his e-devotionals to seventy-five family members and friends, who forward them along to others.

Just think of the ripples—the many lives that are being impacted by a father's simple messages to his son in college. And it all began during a rather common transition in a couple's life, when they brought their cares before the Lord in prayer.

PRAYER EXERCISE

PUTTING FEET TO YOUR PRAYERS

Pray together for your children, whether they are still under your roof, away at college, or living on their own. As you intercede for them, ask God if there is some tangible way that He would have you encourage them, and let them know that you're praying. Or ask Him for a creative way to share His Word with them. Perhaps you could send a care package of goodies that includes some kind of fruit bread and a verse like "I am the Bread of Life." Or you could write down all the Scriptures you've prayed for your children during the semester. Persevere in prayer for them, and then watch what the Lord does in their lives and in your own.

Praying on the Hill

I urge, then, first of all, that requests, prayers,

intercession and thanksgiving

be made for everyone—for kings and all those in authority,

that we may live peaceful and quiet lives in all godliness and holiness.

This is good, and pleases God our Savior, who wants all men

to be saved and to come to a knowledge of the truth.

1 TIMOTHY 2:1–4

When Roger and Lin Story visited Washington, D.C., in 1981, their lives changed in one single moment. Standing outside the door of the Russell Senate Office Building, they watched a well-known senator walk by. Roger felt God speak clearly to his heart: "You have never prayed for that man."

This was true, Roger and Lin realized. They had prayed at him. They had prayed against him. They had even prayed that the senator would be removed from office. But they had never prayed *for* him. That day they began to pray together for this senator. Through this single incident, God began to show them how to pray with love, compassion, and insight for the leaders of our nation, state, city, and churches.

The Storys took that lesson with them back to the California church they pastored and began to teach the people in their congregation how to pray for America. They continued to pray for this senator and for the nation's leaders. They prayed such prayers every week. Soon they saw God work in many areas of leadership. Christian leaders began to be drawn to their church. Their young people were elected to student body offices. The Storys found that the local school board was willing to listen to them simply because the board members knew that they prayed regularly for them.

Lin also began to encourage teachers in their Christian school to lead the kids in prayer for the nation's leaders. Children from one third-grade class began to pray regularly for a member of the Reagan administration. One day this leader came to visit the class. He sat in one of the small chairs as the kids gathered around him. As they prayed about things he assumed nobody knew about, he began to weep. A year later at a meeting in Washington, Lin heard this man talk about the most profound intercessors he'd ever met—a group of third graders!

On another occasion, Lin brought a newspaper article into the prekindergarten classroom and encouraged the children to pray for Albert, the son of Senator Al Gore. Albert lay in the hospital with critical injuries after being hit by a car on his way to a baseball game. The young students and their teacher prayed fervently and then wrote cards

We must accept God's sovereign purpose in having placed leaders in authority, and pray for them with a loving heart, believing, as we do, that God is working.

JOY DAWSON

To clasp the hands in prayer is the beginning of an uprising against the disorder of the world.

KARL BARTH

of encouragement to the Gore family. Their prayers reached heaven and touched God's heart. Albert and his family received the marvelous healing grace of God.

Inspired by the children's desire to join in praying for national leaders, Lin founded the National Children's Prayer Network to train kids in intercession, guide them into prayer for our nation and its leaders, and help them find their destiny in Christ.

The next step was an even bigger one. In 1989, God impressed Roger and Lin to move their ministry from California to Washington, D.C. Their step of faith was confirmed as doors opened for ministry in the lives of senators and representatives, ambassadors, and international diplomats.

Still, they encountered huge obstacles. Roger and Lin had to work together to find housing, a church home, a high school for their two teenagers, and financial support for the ministry and for their family's needs. They faced challenging times. Scary times, such as the day the car in which they had been riding just moments before exploded into flames. Anxious times, when financial needs loomed like darkness in their minds. And discouraging times, like the day Lin learned that she would have to pack up and move once again because the place they were house-sitting had just been sold.

We are working with God to determine the future! Certain things will happen in history if we pray rightly. We are to change the world by prayer.

RICHARD FOSTER

Roger and Lin have spent countless hours in prayer together throughout Washington—at the Capitol building, the White House, the Supreme Court, and many other places in the city. During one three-month period, they walked the ten blocks to the White House every night, stood at the massive iron gate, and prayed for the president. They sought God's heart for this leader and asked Him how He wanted them to pray. Night after night, they interceded, pouring out their hearts in prayer for him. A few months later, while their children were praying at the White House, a White House staffer invited Roger and Lin inside to visit with the president. There they were able to share God's love and truth with him.

Wherever they are, they work closely as a team. Lin's National Children's Prayer Network and Prayer Congress (where kids from around the country come together for teaching, fellowship, and prayer for America during National Day of Prayer week) complements Roger's work on the Hill, the National Leadership Ministries.[5] Although Roger's ministry must keep a low profile, the children's prayer ministry is well known on the Hill and at the White House.

As Roger and Lin continue to pray, doors continue to open for God to enter the hearts of the men and women who lead our nation. They ministered to the ambassador from Kuwait during the Gulf War and have spoken in numerous churches to encourage Christians to pray for our country. They facilitate the ministry to children when kids come to Washington every year to pray for our national leaders. As Lin and the children have met with the president, vice president, ambassadors, legislators, and staff members, the Storys have seen the power of God's Word as it is sown in the hearts of leaders, the heart of our nation.

All because a couple prayed!

What God wills to accomplish on earth needs prayer as its indispensable condition. And there is but one way for Christ and believers. A heart and mouth open toward heaven in believing prayer will certainly not be put to shame!

ANDREW MURRAY

PRAYER EXERCISE
HISTORY-SHAPING PRAYER

Roger and Lin have found that one of the keys to their ministry is to "keep showing up" for prayer—to persevere. This might simply mean being where they need to be at the right moment and doing what God shows them to do. Whether writing a letter of encouragement or meeting with an ambassador or the president, they see God use their simple efforts to change lives.

Is God calling *you* to pray for a senator, congressman, or some other national leader? Perhaps He wants you to be an intercessor for the governor, local mayor, or even the school board president. Ask Him to show you which people in power need your prayers the most—then pray faithfully for those leaders.

- Pray for him or her to make wise decisions.
- Pray for his or her family, for God's blessing, for unity and mutual support in love.
- Pray for godly counselors to be placed around the leader, and if he or she doesn't know Christ personally, for laborers to be sent to share the truth and lead him or her to God.

Prayer Works!

Don't be weary in prayer; keep at it;

watch for God's answers and remember to be thankful

when they come.

COLOSSIANS 4:2, TLB

In Jesus' name, amen. Karen looked up and smiled.

A deep sense of satisfaction filled Doug's heart as he returned her smile and held her hand. At her suggestion, they had just spent an hour praying together as husband and wife for the first time in years. They had prayed for each of their four children, for unsaved family members, for friends who were having marital problems, and for their own marriage and relationships with the Lord.

Why haven't we been doing this all along? Doug thought.

He remembers that night several years ago as the beginning of their regular Sunday night prayer time. And what a difference it has made! Doug and Karen have come to believe that prayer between a husband and wife is the most powerful resource God gives to every Christian couple. They've seen firsthand that prayer *works!*

Because Karen is at home with small children and Doug works with international students on a university campus, it would be easy for them to get disconnected from each other. But as Doug and Karen pray for their kids and for their international friends, their hearts are drawn into a common purpose and vision. The result? A deeper involvement in each other's lives, deeper appreciation and understanding of what each is doing, and a continuous sparkle in their marriage.

Prayer is like a splint that binds two hearts together and makes them one.

DOUG WENDEL

See to it that you pray for your children. Then you will leave them a great legacy of answers to prayer, which will follow them all the days of their life.

O. HALLESBY

They've also seen God move in the lives of their children. Their youngest daughter, Danielle, was two years old when Doug and Karen began praying together regularly. Danielle was a sweet but strong-willed, do-her-own-thing kind of child who often responded to her parents' requests and discipline with lengthy screaming fits. Doug and Karen began praying that God would give Danielle a desire to obey them and the authorities He placed in her life.

Sometimes it seemed as if their prayers were bouncing off the ceiling, because their daughter's difficult behavior continued. But they kept praying and working with Danielle, and, after some months, they began to see some positive changes in her attitude. One day after he asked her to pick up her toys, Doug braced himself for another bout of opposition. Imagine his surprise when Danielle replied, "Okay, Daddy!"

Danielle is now six, and her parents continue to pray for God to shape her strong will and use it for her good and His purposes.

Seeing God work in the life of their daughter, Doug was struck with the thought, *If we aren't praying for these needs in our kids, who is?* Nobody. Because nobody knows their children's needs as their parents do. Nobody loves them as their parents do. Nobody else knows their spiritual, character, emotional, and social needs. That thought gave Doug and Karen even more motivation to keep praying—together—for their children.

They've also seen God do some awesome things in response to their prayers for unsaved parents, siblings, nieces, and nephews.

"Why do I need to believe in Jesus?" Karen's father, a South Dakota rancher, asked when they talked to him about the Lord during one visit to the ranch. "Why do I have to go to the hired hand instead of going to the boss man—God?" He didn't see any need for a relationship with Christ and was resistant to the gospel. But Sunday after Sunday, Doug and Karen prayed that Karen's dad would come to know Christ.

Months went by with no obvious changes. What Doug and Karen didn't know was that the rancher had begun reading the Bible. During that time he also survived a battle with cancer. He felt that his life had been spared, and his heart slowly began to change. He began to see his need for Christ. Over a two-year period, as Doug and

When we seek God for answers, we must persevere in prayer, letting it build up day after day until the force of it becomes a mighty tide pushing over all obstacles.

JIM CYMBALA

From the first day that you set your heart to understand, and to humble yourself before God, your words were heard; and I have come because of your words.

DANIEL 10:12, NKJV

Karen continued to pray, her father came to a point of belief and trust in Jesus. What a happy day it was for them when they traveled to South Dakota and Doug baptized his father-in-law.

That glimpse of God's grace keeps them praying for many other family members. This kind of persevering prayer is *work*. Many a time they have been tempted to settle down and watch TV or read a book on Sunday night after they have tucked the kids in bed, instead of interceding for their siblings and parents. But Doug and Karen have seen what an eternal difference prayer makes, and they refuse to give up. They plan to keep praying the rest of their lives. Persevering prayer is work. But is also *works*.

PRAYER EXERCISE
MAKE A DATE FOR PRAYER

Daily prayer together is a great goal, but if it sounds overwhelming, you might try designating a time once each week, as Doug and Karen did. Since so much happens on a weekly basis, it might be more natural for you to have a weekly time to pray as a couple.

First, briefly discuss your children's needs, your unsaved family members, and the needs you each have in your work, daily tasks, or ministry. Then hold hands and bring your needs to God.

When you are just starting out, especially if you aren't used to longer blocks of time, pray for five or ten minutes. Then, as you feel more and more comfortable, increase your time before the Lord together as you praise Him, present your needs and concerns, and listen for His guidance. As you see what He does in your life and marriage, you'll be encouraged to keep it up for the long haul!

A Prayer for
Our Children

Heavenly Father, thank You for our children, gifts from You.
We want them to know You and the power of Your Spirit.
Help us to help them hide Your Word in their hearts at an early age.
Show us what's on Your heart for each child,
so we can pray in agreement with Your will for their lives.
We pray that our children would love
You with all their heart, soul, mind, and strength.
Grant us grace to love them unconditionally
and parent them with wisdom.
Fill our home with joy and let us so live before them
that they will be drawn to Your banquet table.
Amen.

Turning a Prodigal's Heart toward Home

If you know people who have wandered off from God's truth,

don't write them off. Go after them.

Get them back and you will have rescued precious lives

from destruction and prevented an epidemic

of wandering away from God.

JAMES 5:19–20, THE MESSAGE

*L*ike most parents, Brian and Kay had big plans for their children and a vision for the path they would walk in life. But with a will of his own, their much-loved oldest son, Jordan, started down a road much different from the one they had envisioned.

Jordan had always been a high-energy, challenging child. After high school and two wasted semesters at a nearby junior college, he announced, "Dad, I want to be independent; I want some money to strike out on my own. I've got plans."

They didn't have a lot, but Brian gave him some money, and Jordan went off on his own. It wasn't long before he was living on an emotional roller coaster, dependent on alcohol and drugs.

For Brian and Kay, praying together had never been easy, especially after the honeymoon phase of their marriage ended and they began to discover each other's faults. How could they join hands and hearts in such a holy act, knowing that they were so far from being holy themselves? Praying together felt almost hypocritical.

But desperate times call for desperate measures, and when Jordan went off the deep end, their concern for him kept Brian and Kay on their knees.

Soon they heard from one of his friends that, with only five dollars in his pocket, Jordan had hitchhiked to California—alone. They didn't know where he was or if they would ever see him again. But one night they received a phone call. Their son was homeless, hungry, and (they thought) humbled.

Whether the prodigal you're praying for is a child, a sibling, a parent, a spouse—whoever it might be—eventually you must put him or her in God's hands and trust Him to do a work of grace in that person's life.

Q U I N   S H E R R E R

"Could I come home?" he wanted to know. "And would you wire me a plane ticket?"

How could they refuse? *Lord, be with our child. Be His shepherd and bring this lost sheep back to You and to us. And help him know the difference between pig slop and home cooking. Turn his heart toward home!*

All the way to the airport, Brian and Kay prayed that God would show them what to say and do. They asked God for a breakthrough to change Jordan's heart.

But, unlike the prodigal son of the Bible, Jordan's heart didn't change. When Brian and Kay looked into the eyes of their son, someone they had never met looked back at them. His mind simply wasn't the same. The drugs he had used had robbed them of Jordan. *Where's our* son? *Lord, what's happened to him?* they asked. The power of the drugs and the battle for his mind and soul staggered them.

A few days after he arrived home, Jordan broke into a rage and destroyed everything in sight. Later he broke out their van window and the door of their house. It took a restraining order to protect their other children and their home from his rages. Next came a round of professionals—three different counselors and a psychologist. Their diagnosis was *bipolar, manic state;* their prescription, *long-term medication.* But Jordan refused to take it.

When you're afraid for your child, you try many things. At first you might rely on wise people, counselors, tough love, and other strategies for change. In fact, you'll try everything you can think of. But, in time, you reach the point of feeling totally helpless. When you come to the end of your resources, you simply pray. That's where Brian and Kay found themselves over and over— broken and helpless, on their knees before God.

Intercessory prayer for one who is sinning prevails. God says so! The will of the one prayed for does not come into question at all; he is connected with God by prayer, and prayer on the basis of the Redemption sets the connection working and God gives life.

OSWALD CHAMBERS

There were times when they felt as though they were in a fog. It was hard to read Scripture and even harder to pray. Yet they needed God's Word and were desperate for Him to move in their lives and in the life of their son. Like the paralytic who couldn't walk to Jesus, sometimes they had to rely on each other or on their friends to carry them to God's throne on the mattress of prayer. Knowing that they weren't the only ones praying encouraged their hearts. Both sets of grandparents and many others were covering Jordan in prayer, storming heaven on his behalf.

Once, after taking someone else's medication, Jordan had a seizure at a bus station. Kay was torn up, discouraged that God wasn't moving faster in her son's life. Brian intervened. "Hon, we're becoming obsessed. Jordan's all we talk about. We're neglecting our other three kids. We've got to leave him in God's hands." So they put Jordan on the back burner to let God stir the pot of his life. They entrusted to God the child they couldn't seem to reach.

They continued to pray for their wayward child, but they also went on with their own lives. As they reminded each other that God wouldn't forget Jordan, they gradually found a measure of peace—not complete peace—but enough to go on, to enjoy their other children, and to take care of their responsibilities.

The next few months were their worst. From week to week, they did not know what Jordan would do. Then the downward spiral began to even out. Scared by hallucinations and seizures, Jordan backed off marijuana and other drugs. As he gradually became drug free, his mind became clearer. His erratic behavior began to stabilize. His depression slowly started to lift.

Jordan's life still isn't all together. His parents still don't have all the

Never underestimate the power that comes when a parent pleads with God on behalf of a child.

MAX LUCADO

A small prayer answered is an encouragement to keep the spiritual lights on, to keep praying, to keep loving even when we feel unsure any of it will change the situation.

VALERIE AND
STEVE BELL

answers, and they are still praying. But shafts of light are gleaming through the darkness. Small prayers are being answered, which gives them hope. And Scripture reminds them that God, who began a good work in their son when he was a little boy, will complete it in His time (Philippians 1:6). Brian and Kay know that even before they loved their son, God loved him...and that God loves Jordan even more than they do. Jordan has a future and a hope, and they will pray until it arrives!

PRAYER EXERCISE
PRAYING SCRIPTURE FOR YOUR CHILD

The Bible is an ideal prayer manual for couples. When you pray Scripture, you use passages of God's Word to form prayers. When you pray a verse back to God, it becomes the cry of your own heart, and you can be assured that you're praying in God's will. Praying Scripture verses for your child will fill you with confidence and hope. Whether you have a troubled child, as this couple did, or your children are following God, here are some Scriptures to pray for them:

- Pray that each of your children's lives will be a testimony of the love and greatness of Christ. (Philippians 2:15–16; 1 Thessalonians 5:23)
- Pray that the eyes of your child's heart—his spiritual eyes—will be opened and that he'll see God's love for him and the hope of His calling. (Ephesians 1:17–18)
- Pray that your child will be hedged in so that he can't find his way to the wrong people or places—and that the wrong people can't find their way to him. (Hosea 2:6)
- Pray that he will be caught when guilty. (Psalm 119:71)
- Pray that your child will learn to submit to God, drawing near to Him and resisting Satan. (James 4:7)

Praying the Wrong Mate out the Door

When two of you get together on anything at all on earth

and make a prayer of it, my Father in heaven goes into action.

MATTHEW 18:19, *THE MESSAGE*

One summer night when our oldest son, Justin, was home from college, Holmes and I sat on our bed discussing the young woman who had recently come crashing into Justin's life. He was out past his curfew—again—and we were weary of waiting up for him yet another night.

Just a week earlier, Justin and Carey (not her real name) had gone to Tulsa to a reggae festival. Justin had called us in the middle of the night to tell us he wouldn't be coming home until morning. "It's just too late to drive home and we're tired. Don't worry; we'll sleep in different beds. I'll see you tomorrow!" he said, hanging up the phone.

Justin had met Carey the first summer weekend he was back home from his freshman year of college. She was cute and perky—dark hair and eyes, an engaging smile—and she had obviously won a place in Justin's heart, if not in ours. After that first night, they were practically inseparable. As they continued to date and spend long periods of time together, we began to see red flags in Carey's life. We also noticed how she was influencing our son, and our concerns mounted.

Carey's parents, who both had been divorced and remarried a couple of times, lived in a different state. They had set her up in her own apartment when she was eighteen. Since she planned to return to college in the fall after her summer "break," she didn't have a job. With her own place, unlimited money, a new car, and no responsibilities, Carey had a lot of time on her hands. She wasn't a Christian, and soon drinking and partying began to dominate her nights. Our son joined Carey in her pursuit of fun.

> *There is never panic in heaven!... You can only hold on to that reality through faith because it...often seems as if the devil is the victor. But God is faithful and His plans never fail!*
>
> CORRIE TEN BOOM

After Carey had declined numerous invitations to our family dinners, Sunday lunches, and birthday celebrations, it dawned on us that *family* was a bad word to her. She avoided any gatherings that included parents.

The more we voiced our concerns and tried to talk some sense into Justin, the more he seemed magnetized to the girl. We asked him to consider whether Carey was the type of girl he would want to marry, and we reminded him that the Bible told us not to be yoked together with unbelievers.

He assured us that he wanted to help her and that he felt she needed his support and understanding because she was from a dysfunctional family. While Justin seemed sure he could fix Carey's problems, he became more and more entangled in what, to us, looked like a negative, codependent relationship that was leading him in the wrong direction. Carey didn't want to attend church, so Justin didn't either. He had almost no time to be with our family, and he lost touch with old friends who didn't run in her circles.

All our attempts failed to persuade Justin that Carey was a bad influence. We thought he should break up with her, but he wouldn't listen to us.

Meanwhile, I prayed frantically for Justin and searched for other prayer warriors to join me in spiritual battle. I spent many mornings on my knees asking God to turn our son around, but as the Oklahoma sun blazed and the summer days got hotter, Carey and Justin seemed almost cemented together. I grew discouraged and weary.

One day as Holmes and I hashed over the problem, it finally occurred to us that we had been praying for Justin individually, but not together as a couple. Suddenly we both felt an urgency to join forces and storm heaven on Justin's behalf.

Prayer is of transcendent importance.... Prayer succeeds when all else fails.

E. M. BOUNDS

We decided to seek counsel from our pastor, who happened to be the father of nine children, eight of whom were girls. He told us about all the boyfriends he and his wife had prayed "out the door" and suggested that we pray a "hedge of thorns" prayer based on Hosea 2:6–7. In these verses, Hosea says that he will block his straying wife's path with thorn bushes and wall her in so that even if she chases after her lovers, she won't catch them, and they won't find her.

Our pastor encouraged us to ask God to remove Carey from Justin's life and wall them away from each other if this girl wasn't who God intended to be our son's lifelong partner.

"You mean this is 'legal'—a biblical prayer?" I asked.

He assured me that it was. "And from the looks of the situation, you'd better start praying it soon," he added.

As Holmes and I prayed, we were both assured that Justin's relationship with Carey was a youthful folly rather than a direction in which

God was leading him. We asked God to separate Justin and Carey. We also asked that if he persisted in the relationship, everywhere he turned he would run into a barrier and that he would lose interest in her as quickly as he had fallen for her.

Lord, if this girl is Your choice for our son, then we ask You to rescue her out of darkness and bring her into Your marvelous light and give us a real love for her. Whatever happens, Lord, we pray for her salvation, that she would know Your love and commit her life to You. But if she's not Your plan for Justin, please separate them and cause them to lose interest in each other.

It took a lot of faith to pray the "lose interest in each other" part of the prayer because from all appearances, they seemed increasingly enthralled with each other. But Holmes and I were on the same page with what we were asking God for, and that night we entrusted our son into His hands, trusting Him to work it all out in His own way and His own time.

At first the situation only seemed to get worse. The very next week Carey talked Justin into transferring to her university. He informed us that they were going there to check things out and to get him enrolled. She had even selected a place for him to live—the garage apartment behind her place, if it were still available.

Needless to say, I was more than a little concerned over this turn of events. But as Holmes and I continued praying together, we felt that we should not forbid the trip, even though we were afraid that it might push him further into her arms. Instead, we offered for one of us to go along. As we talked with Justin, we tried to hold a mirror in front of him that would reflect the wrong choices he was making. We hoped that a turnaround would come from within him instead of from our trying to coerce him to our way of thinking. Justin agreed to take one of us along and, since Holmes had to be at the construction site where he was working, I went.

Monday morning, Carey's car zoomed out of our driveway. I sat in the back seat, feeling like an intruder and trying to keep my mouth shut. I concentrated on trying to be pleasant, and I prayed silently every moment of the trip. As we approached the campus, Carey talked about how much fun it would be when they could eat breakfast together, go to class together, eat lunch together, and study together. That sounded like an awful lot of togetherness to me!

After our arrival in Stillwater, Justin and Carey headed to a real estate office for a list of apartments and then drove around in the August heat to look into several possibilities. Then they made their way to registration to check on available classes. No courses were open in Justin's major. He could take some electives that wouldn't count toward his major, but it would mean that he would graduate a semester late. Justin and Carey checked a few more apartments, then discovered that the garage apartment behind Carey's place had been rented. The day had been a total bust. I breathed a sigh of relief. *Thank you, Lord.* Carey made plans to return the following week to find Justin an apartment and see if any classes had opened up.

Understand what the Lord's will is.

EPHESIANS 5:17, NKJV

That night at dinner, Justin told Holmes and me that he still wanted to transfer to OSU. Calmly, we replied that he could transfer if he wanted to but that we simply could not financially support it because the transfer wouldn't advance his progress toward a degree. He had already registered for courses at OU and had signed a lease on a nice apartment. We'd be glad to continue paying for his education there, we said.

Instead of putting up a fight, Justin thought about it and decided to return to OU.

After school started and Carey had returned to her university, Justin quickly lost interest in her and began dating another girl. After a few phone calls, the relationship faded quickly. God had heard us and answered our prayers!

What's more, at the end of that school year Justin recommitted his life to Christ. The next year he met Tiffany, the young woman God had prepared for him to marry. Interestingly, one night when I was talking to Tiffany's mom during the course of their engagement, she told me about "praying the wrong guy out the door" of her daughter's life. It had happened at approximately the same time that Holmes and I had been praying our own, similar prayer.

PRAYER EXERCISE
PRAYING IN AGREEMENT

One of the most powerful prayers for bringing about change is the prayer of agreement as expressed in Matthew 18:19–20. Read this verse together, and then think of a situation that's been troubling you or your family. Ask God for His perspective and how He would want you to pray. Discuss and pray about it until you are both in agreement about how to proceed. Then when you're in harmony, give that petition to God and stand on the promise of this passage. Write down your prayer so you can keep asking, seeking, and knocking—and when the answer comes, remember to thank God for how He worked.

In His Name

It is God himself who has made us what we are

and given us new lives from Christ Jesus;

and long ages ago he planned that we should spend these lives

in helping others.

EPHESIANS 2:10, TLB

"Daddy, Jesus forgives you, and I forgive you for divorcing Mom," seventeen-year-old Julie told her father one day as they were talking on the phone.

Dee, Julie's father, and Margaret, his new wife, had never been a churchgoing couple. Having divorced their spouses, they had married each other four years earlier. Yet they still were not happy, and selfishness and guilt over what they'd done to their families left their marriage in turmoil.

That simple declaration of forgiveness from Dee's daughter began to open their hearts. Whereas before they had rolled their eyes or silently scoffed when televangelists preached, now they began to be open to the gospel. Before long, Dee got a Bible and began to read it at lunch. He also listened to Bible study programs on the radio as he traveled the highways in his sales job for an industrial chemical company.

Within three months of his daughter's call, Dee and Margaret gave their lives to Christ. Suddenly their perspective on everything changed.

Excited about their new life in Christ, they began to pray together. The Scriptures came alive to them, and God seemed to be summoning them to action.

Two passages in particular struck them. The first was Ephesians 2:8–10: "For it is by grace you have been saved, through faith—and this not from yourselves, it is the gift of God—not by works, so that no one can boast. For we are God's workmanship, created in Christ Jesus to do good works, which God prepared in advance for us to do."

As we pray for the needy around us, God may open our eyes to what we can do to help in immediate need. He may use us as an answer to our own prayers.

EDITH SCHAEFFER

Created to do good works. As Dee and Margaret pondered this, another translation helped clarify God's intention for them: "Long ages ago he planned that we should spend these lives in helping others" (v. 10, TLB).

The second verse that struck them was Matthew 18:19–20: "Again, I tell you that if two of you on earth agree about anything you ask for, it will be done for you by my Father in heaven. For where two or three come together *in my name,* there am I with them" (emphasis added).

Dee and Margaret discovered that, in marriage, the couple and Christ are a unit created to fulfill what God has prepared for them to do. They were excited to realize that this was their destiny as Christians. They also realized that God promised them a special effectiveness when they agreed together in His name about what they were asking.

When they read "Your kingdom come. Your will be done, on earth as it is in heaven" (Matthew 6:10, NASB), Dee and Margaret longed to know specifically how they could be a part of God's will on earth. They weren't sure how to do it yet, but with Christ's help, they wanted to serve others.

Motivated by their desire to serve God totally, Dee and Margaret decided to fast for a week and ask for His guidance. Every morning when they woke up, they asked, "What do you want us to do today, Lord? Guide us. Use us, Father."

One day, only a few hours after they had made that request, Dee was at Children's Hospital visiting the child of one of his customers. On his way out, he called Margaret from the phone in the chaplain's office.

"Billy, the little boy we prayed for in church, is at Children's too," Margaret told him. The seven-year-old had been hit by a pickup truck and was in a coma. "As long as you're there, why don't you go by and see how he's doing?"

Overhearing their conversation, the priest in the chaplain's office said, "I'll take you right up there," and escorted Dee to the pediatric intensive care unit.

Dee gently placed his hand on Billy's arm and prayed a simple prayer for the comatose boy. His heart also went out to the other critically ill kids he saw in the unit, and he started to pray for them too, but at that moment there was a code blue on a child, and a doctor quickly ushered Dee out of the room.

If we have God-given compassion and concern for others, our faith will grow and strengthen as we pray. In fact, if we genuinely love people, we desire for them far more than it is within our power to give, and that will cause us to pray.

RICHARD FOSTER

When he stepped into the hall, Billy's parents and grandparents saw him. "Would you pray with us?" they asked. Dee prayed and cried with the heartbroken family of the little boy.

Dee and Margaret continued to pray for Billy, and two days later Dee was again at Children's Hospital. The first person he ran into was the priest.

"There's that man who knows how to pray good prayers!" the chaplain exclaimed. He went on to say that Billy had come out of the coma twenty minutes after Dee's prayer. The priest added that Billy had had successful surgery to remove his spleen and that he was now in a regular room, with his broken leg in traction. Dee visited Billy and thanked God for His mercy on this young boy.

Around us is a world lost in sin, above us is a God willing and able to save; it is ours to build the bridge that links heaven and earth, and prayer is the mighty instrument that does the work.

E. M. BOUNDS

Almost every day, Dee and Margaret continued to ask God, "What do you want us to do?" Again and again, God seemed to guide them to local hospitals. Dee was still working at his sales job in the daytime, while Margaret worked full time in a dentist's office. But in the evenings and on weekends, they followed the Spirit's nudging. One evening they might visit the surgical waiting area at Presbyterian Hospital; another time they'd drop in on the intensive care unit at Mercy. Soon they were visiting over a hundred patients!

They learned to be flexible and to do what God showed them. Often their ministry started as casually as approaching someone in the waiting room and asking, "Is there someone I could be praying for?" or "Is there a need I could pray with you about?" In hundreds of encounters, no one ever turned down their invitation, and they touched many lives.

As Dee and Margaret continued their hospital ministry, they came across many people with financial needs—people with a child in the hospital but no money for meals or a hotel room nearby; people whose electricity or gas had been turned off; people who had lost their jobs; and people with mounting medical bills and no money to pay them.

One night they took groceries to the home of a single mother with four kids. There were so many holes in the wall that they could almost see right through it. The kids were crying, and there was no heat to warm them. The kitchen was infested with cockroaches. Overwhelmed by it all, Dee and Margaret simply handed the mother the sacks of groceries and started to leave.

"Aren't you going to pray for me?" the mother asked them.

Of course they stopped, visited with the mother and her children, and prayed with them.

That experience taught Dee and Margaret to keep one ear open to the person in need and the other ear open to the Lord so that they could hear how He wanted them to help. They found that as they did this, they could bring hope to seemingly hopeless situations. They learned to focus not on holes in the wall or cockroaches in the kitchen, but on the people themselves and how they could bring Christ's love to them. Over and over they found that their words about God's love were

The trouble with nearly everybody who prays is that he says "Amen" and runs away before God has a chance to reply. Listening to God is far more important than giving him your ideas.

FRANK LAUBACH

more credible when they were accompanied by a tangible response to people's needs.

Word of their outreach spread quickly, and Dee and Margaret began to get more calls for help. They counseled and prayed with disabled people, the elderly, and any hurting person God brought their way. Eventually they wondered if God wanted them to leave their jobs and serve Him full time. They had no funds, no savings, and no support group to back them, but their desire to go full time grew increasingly stronger. When they described their plans to their friends at church, most of them just smiled or made a polite remark. Leaving their livelihoods to minister full time simply was not a logical thing to do!

Apart from the confidence God gave them, there was no reason for them to hope for success. Nevertheless, Dee and Margaret gave notice at their jobs and began In His Name Ministries, Inc.[6] From the start, their ministry brought them great joy, even though the early years were financially difficult. For a long time, Dee and Margaret were as poor as some of the people they helped. They often talked about one of them returning to a "regular" job, but every time they considered throwing in the towel, God would do something to keep them going.

For example, one Saturday a year after they started their ministry, Margaret was praying for their financial needs as she worked in the yard. She cried out, *Lord, if money doesn't come by Monday, I am going to get a job.* Twenty minutes later a friend called to say that she and her husband had been praying and had decided to send them a thousand dollars from their savings account. "Something made me call you *now* and tell you our intentions," the woman said.

Today more than four hundred individuals and thirteen churches support the work of In His Name Ministries. Each day, Dee and Margaret receive more than forty calls for help. For several years a Christian radio station gave them free radio time. Later, another station provided spot announcements to remind people of opportunities to help someone in need. Dee and Margaret send a monthly newsletter to people they know, but they have never engaged in fund-raising efforts. And since 1996, the IHN Web site has helped them expand their original boundaries. As this chapter was being written, a family in Redmond, Washington, sent a check for five hundred dollars to be applied to the expenses of a family in Edmond, Oklahoma, whose young son is battling a fast-spreading cancer.

As Dee and Margaret have continued to ask that simple question, "Lord, what do you want us to do today?" and serve Him through this ministry of compassion, their marriage has been enriched beyond their wildest dreams. As they have given and refreshed others, God has refreshed them and poured countless blessings upon their family. God has truly done more than they could have thought or prayed or imagined, according to His riches and glory in Christ Jesus (Ephesians 3:20–21).

PRAYER EXERCISE

A PRAYER EXPERIMENT

When you wake up each morning, ask God together, "What do you want us to do today? How can we serve You? How can we be Your hands and feet to touch lives?" Then, whether at home or at work, follow His gentle nudges as you go through your day. Try this for a month, and compare notes regularly to see what happens as you pray and follow God's leading.

A Morning Prayer

Lord, as this day begins, we don't know what's going to come our way
or even what the next few hours will hold.
But this is the day that You have made, and we want to
rejoice and be glad in it!
And before we start our work or tasks,
we want to put ourselves at Your disposal
and surrender our lives to You anew.
Since we know that without You we can accomplish nothing,
help us abide in You just as a branch abides in the vine.
Help us draw strength from You throughout the day.
Fill our minds with Your thoughts and ideas.
We want to trust You and turn to You in every time of stress.
Lord, You are the water of life.
As this day begins, fill us with Your Spirit!
Show us how we can serve You!
And let our lives overflow with praise to You and love for others.
Amen.

Do Your Kids Know When You Pray?

I have called daily upon You.

PSALM 88:9, NKJV

"ould you get Mom on the other phone so I can talk to both of you?" Chuck and Pat's youngest son asked his dad.

Scott was calling from the seafood restaurant across the street from the high school he attended. Just like his older brothers, he bused tables there evenings and Saturdays to pay for the upkeep on the used car his folks had given him when he turned sixteen.

The couple's thoughts ran wild during the few seconds it took Pat to get to the phone. In fact, their hearts were in their throats. Chuck and Pat were home alone that night, and when the hour struck eight, they had gone to their bedroom to pray—as had been their practice for the past several years. They almost never answered the telephone when they were praying. However, this time when the phone rang, they looked at each other and said, "We should answer this call."

"I can't believe you answered the phone," Scott said, "but I'm sure glad you did."

"What's going on, son?"

"I hurt my back real bad," he replied, gasping for breath. "I mean real bad. So bad I can hardly walk, and I can't stand up straight at all. Pain is shooting up my spine. A guy who works with me helped me to the phone and dialed the number."

Chuck said, "Scott, do you want us to call an ambulance or pick you up and take you to the hospital?"

"We can be there in no time," Pat added. "I'll call Dr. Spears and have him meet us there."

"No. Don't call an ambulance or come get me," Scott replied. "I was picking up a big pan loaded with dirty dishes, and my back just snapped. I couldn't stand up straight. I could barely move. I looked down at my watch, and I knew it was your prayer time. I only called to see if you could pray for me. I know if you do that, I'll be okay."

Chuck and Pat still felt that they should pick up their son and take him to the emergency room. But Scott insisted that they pray.

"Of course we'll pray for you," Pat assured him, "but if you need us to come and get you and your car, call us, and we'll be right there."

After hanging up the phone, the couple prayed that God would heal

Fortunate are they whose fathers and mothers have left them a wealthy patrimony of prayer.

E. M. BOUNDS

The Christian life rooted in the secret place where God meets and walks and talks with his own grows into such a testimony of Divine power that all men will feel its influence and be touched by the warmth of its love.

E. M. BOUNDS

Scott's back—align every vertebra, relax every muscle, and ease the pain—and let Scott stand pain free before his fellow workers as a testimony to the wonderful God who loves him.

Although the two hours until Scott arrived home seemed more like two days, at 10:00 P.M. he strode into the house with a big smile on his face. He told his parents how awestruck the other high school and college workers had been at what had taken place that evening.

Prayer—since it is an act of hope and trust—fosters peace in the midst of crisis.

A R T   H U N T

Within ten minutes after he asked his parents to pray, Scott's pain disappeared. He stood perfectly straight and went back to work at full tilt. Actually, Scott may have been the only employee working after that, because his coworkers were all watching him in amazement and talking about the fact that Scott had "just wanted to call his parents to have them pray for him."

If as parents we do not make pursuing God a priority, it will not happen for our families.

B I L L   C A R M I C H A E L

Today Scott's back remains strong and straight. Now he and his wife and brothers and their spouses call Chuck and Pat regularly with various prayer requests—for themselves as well as for their children, other family members, and friends. They know that Chuck and Pat keep a regular appointment with God every evening. Sometimes these family members show up unexpectedly at 8:00 P.M. to ask for or receive prayer. What a bond has developed as this family has discovered the power of praying together!

PRAYER EXERCISE
DO YOUR KIDS KNOW THAT YOU'RE PRAYING?

For a creative way to let your children or grandchildren know that you are praying for them, get stiff colored paper from the copy shop and trace their handprints on the paper. In the middle of each hand, write a Scripture verse that you've chosen to pray for each child. While you trace their hands, explain that you have a special time in which you pray for them. Let them know that even when you are not with them, you will put your hand on their handprints to connect with them as you pray.

Clinging to Jesus

And I pray that Christ will be more and more

at home in your hearts,

living within you as you trust in Him.

Ephesians 3 : 17 , tlb

During the years they were raising their family, Jack and Kathleen didn't set aside a specific time to pray together until their children were teenagers. Outside of family devotions, they would pray when a specific need or problem arose. But sometime during their children's adolescent years they began praying together at bedtime, and they've been doing it ever since.

They were especially glad for regular times of prayer together as, one by one their daughters married and started their own families. They recall in particular how their bedtime prayers helped them when their oldest daughter, Lindsay, set out on her own.

Lindsay was a bubbly people person and a vibrant Christian. Although she dated many "up and coming" guys, she was just as often attracted to the "down and outers." After graduating from high school and spending a year in Bible college, she went to work at a church camp. There she met Rick, a new Christian who was ten years her senior. Rick was divorced with four children and had a history of drug abuse.

Over and over again, Lindsay's relationship with Rick drove Jack and Kathleen to their knees. Lindsay had always been a cooperative child, and she valued her parents' opinions. But she had fallen hopelessly in love, and everything they said fell on deaf ears. Her parents pleaded with her, cried, and even gave her lists of reasons why the relationship wouldn't work.

Finally, Lindsay agreed to leave the camp for six months and share an apartment with her younger sister, Jessica, who was engaged to be married.

Surely, the hundred-mile distance will help cool off their relationship, her parents thought. Instead, absence only made Lindsay and Rick's hearts grow fonder.

After her sister's wedding, Lindsay lined up a job and a place to live in a city only thirty miles from the camp. Jack and Kathleen took this new challenge to the Lord. They thought that He was answering their prayers when both the new job and the apartment fell through at the last minute. Lindsay, however, soon left to house-sit at a pastor's home and baby-sit for another family in order to stay close to Rick.

A turning point came a few months later when Jack and Kathleen took a camping vacation about sixty miles from where Lindsay was living. When they arrived at the campsite, they were so burdened for their daughter that all they could do was talk about her situation.

Prayer is putting oneself in the hands of God, at his disposition, and listening to his voice in the depths of our hearts.

MOTHER TERESA

"When you strip everything away, what is the *one thing* we desire for our daughters most of all?" Kathleen finally asked Jack. After a lot of discussion, they agreed that they wanted their girls to marry Christian men who loved God and were serving Him—men who could provide for the girls and who would love and cherish them.

It occurred to them, though, that many marriages starting with all those distinct advantages still failed. They continued to think about the issue. *What is the one most important desire we have for our daughters?* After a lot more discussion, they finally arrived at the bottom line: *Whatever in life will keep them clinging to Jesus.*

With this realization, Jack and Kathleen surrendered Lindsay to the Lord, along with all their hopes and dreams for her. As they did, they experienced a very real sense of peace.

Two days later, Lindsay joined her parents for the day at their campsite. She poured out her heart, sharing how *just two days before* she had been ready to give everything up, including her relationship with Rick, and move back home.

*Unanswered yet? But you
     are not unheeded;*

*The promises of God forever
     stand;*

*To Him our days and years
     alike are equal.*

*Have faith in God! It is your
     Lord's command.*

OPHELIA G. BROWNING

"Everything fell apart," Lindsay explained. "My house-sitting arrangement was about to expire. I had to give up the baby-sitting job and couldn't find a new job or another place to live. You know what, though? The next day things turned around! I found a good job at the credit union and an apartment to rent in the home of a Christian couple. I even found a church I like. Isn't God good? Now I can still be close to Rick!"

At first their hearts sank. *Why did we pray that prayer of surrender?* But they couldn't help recognizing God's sovereign hand and perfect timing. They did not understand the situation, but they trusted God.

Their trust was challenged during Lindsay's engagement. When Kathleen visited Lindsay to help plan the wedding, she found her cooking a big kettle of soup in the kitchen of Rick's tiny trailer, which was in total disarray. Rick had no running water, there was laundry flung over the outside line, and with his four kids there for the summer, the small space was overflowing. It was not the kind of situation a mother would hope for her soon-to-be-married daughter.

If I am a Christian, I am not set on saving my own skin, but on seeing that the salvation of God comes through me to others, and the great way is by intercession.

OSWALD CHAMBERS

Our Lord never referred to unanswered prayer; He taught that prayers were always answered. He ever implied that prayers were answered rightly because of the Heavenly Father's wisdom.

OSWALD CHAMBERS

Kathleen sobbed all the way to Lindsay's apartment that night. The next morning she made a list: *Twenty Reasons Why This Marriage Will Not Work.* She planned to give it to Lindsay when she arrived home from her job. But then Kathleen sat down with her Bible—and one by one, God erased her arguments and reminded her to trust Him.

After the wedding, Jack and Kathleen's trust was tested again and again. They felt as if they were on a roller coaster, and their hearts often ached for their daughter. Before long it was clear that every ounce of life and joy was leaking out of Lindsay. Rick's behavior seemed erratic, and they sensed that something was wrong, but they didn't know what was going on and felt helpless to know what to do.

One night when Lindsay once again couldn't join the family for a birthday dinner, their middle daughter said tearfully, "We can't just sit back and watch this happen. How will we feel ten years from now if we don't at least try to intervene?" Instead, they prayed, asking God to bring everything to light.

Soon after that, Lindsay discovered from one of her husband's friends that Rick was using drugs again. Within a few weeks she had to separate from him for her own protection. She was forced to keep her whereabouts unknown, and for a time the family feared that Lindsay might become the object of Rick's wrath. Eventually the couple sought help, and ten months later they were reunited.

Through all the ups and downs in the twenty years since, Rick has remained drug free. More importantly, he returned to God and now loves Him with all his heart. Jack and Kathleen have watched their son-in-law grow into a loving, caring husband. With the son they adopted six years ago, Rick and Lindsay serve the Lord in their own way—Rick by sharing God's love and His Word with unchurched friends, and Lindsay in Awana leadership and on the worship team at their church.

PRAYER EXERCISE
RELEASING OUR CHILDREN

Think about it: What is the most important desire you have for your children? Bring that to God as you entrust your kids to Him. Maybe the thought of surrendering your child to God as Jack and Kathleen did sounds strange or scary. Consider, though, that at some time in our children's lives (little by little and also in big watershed moments), we must eventually entrust them to God. Otherwise, we will smother them, cling to them, or try to control them. Today, release each of your children into God's hands, and trust Him to work out His plan in their lives.

God Knows about My List!

For My thoughts are not your thoughts,

neither are your ways My ways, says the Lord.

ISAIAH 55:8, AMP

One spring day a few years ago, Bob came home from work and gave his wife, Patty, the news that his project had been cancelled, leaving him and his entire department without jobs. As they absorbed this upsetting news, they headed out to the front yard to let their two little boys play. Walking along the sidewalk with Andrew, the youngest, in her arms, Patty began to pray.

How could this have happened? her heart cried out to God.

The Lord's response was immediate and crystal clear: "What about your list?" *My list?* Patty asked. *You know about my list?* She almost dropped to her knees right there on the sidewalk with the baby in her arms. At the same time she was processing that thought, God spoke to her heart these comforting words: "I am answering the prayers on your list."

A few weeks before, Bob and Patty had been talking about some problems they just couldn't solve. In spite of their careful budgeting, a few medical bills needed to be paid; the car needed repairs; the house needed paint; the front room needed new carpet; and the air conditioner needed replacing. On top of this, their house had lost significant value in the current housing market.

Patty was growing weary with worry about these burdens. So she and Bob decided to make a list of all their concerns and commit them to prayer. She posted the list on her bathroom mirror and tucked a copy in her purse. Whenever she was plagued with worry, she thought of the list, lifted it to God in a short prayer, and reminded herself that everything was in God's hands. The list had become a helpful weapon in her battle against fear and anxiety.

At that moment there on the sidewalk, Patty didn't see the connection between Bob's being laid off and God addressing the needs on their list. She told Bob what she felt God was saying, but still neither of them understood. Together they thanked the Lord for His curious words to them and went inside to prepare dinner.

Although Bob and Patty didn't know it at the time, that day was the beginning of a long and difficult season in their lives. They endured a full year of uncertainty as Bob worked temporary assignments and

Praying together reminds us that God is in control of everything. We become aware of God's presence because we know that when we pray together, God is in our midst to guide and direct us in the day-to-day workings of our marriage.

BOB AND YVONNE
TURNBULL

Let us endeavor to turn all our household griefs and family torments into occasions of profound worship and loving homage to God.

JOSEPH PARKER

searched for a new position. He sent out résumé after résumé, took short-term opportunities, and declined several offers that didn't seem right or that held little potential for his future.

As difficult as things were, Bob and Patty never missed a paycheck or had an empty refrigerator. Yes, the car limped along, and the house still needed repairs, but the couple became increasingly aware that God had every detail worked out. Their part was to trust Him one day at a time.

Along with the prayers of their family and friends, Bob and Patty's prayers saw them through. While there did indeed seem to be cause for worry and concern, their actual experience was one of peace and a strong sense of God's presence. During that year, Bob also gained the skills he would need to accept the permanent position he ultimately found.

Whatever it is that presses you, go tell your Father; put over the matter into His hand, and so shall you be free from that dividing, perplexing care that the world is full of. When you either do or suffer anything, when you are about any purpose or business, go tell God of it, and acquaint Him with it; even burden Him with it, and you will have no more care, but quiet, sweet diligence in your duty, and dependence on Him for the carriage of your matters.

R. LEIGHTON

The words of assurance that God spoke to Patty's heart on the day Bob lost his job gave both of them the courage to press on and not give in to discouragement. Patty was able to be supportive instead of panicked. She was learning how different God's ways are from our ways. He certainly wasn't doing things as Patty had thought He would. But she came to trust that no matter how long it took Bob to find a permanent job, God was answering *all* the prayers on that list.

The temporary jobs Bob accepted did more than meet their basic needs; through them, God provided for each and every item they had prayed about. The medical bills were paid. The air conditioner lasted another year and was replaced just before the Texas heat set in the following May. They had enough money to paint the house. And they were able to replace the carpet the very day before they moved to Oklahoma City—to a much better job situation for Bob.

A prayerful attitude of thankfulness, no matter what the situation, results in our receiving the unsurpassed peace of God.

JOHN MACARTHUR

By that time, the housing market had improved. They sold the house at the exact time the price rebounded to its original market value. They walked away from it debt free. The receipts for their repairs matched almost to the penny the profit they'd made on the house—plus enough to pay for the transmission on their car, which broke down as they were on their way to close the sale.

When Bob and Patty think about their experience, it inspires them all over again. God was faithful in every detail. Yes, God knew about Patty and Bob's list! And through answering their prayers and meeting their needs, He strengthened their faith in Him and encouraged them to continue praying together whenever they faced concerns or problems. Now every time they tell the story, they're passing on the heritage of faith to their sons.

PRAYER EXERCISE

MAKE A LIST

Making a list of your concerns, needs, or worries can be a handle that helps you lay hold of God's provision. Commit your list to prayer together, entrusting each issue to God. Whenever you begin to worry about those needs or concerns, remind yourself: God can handle your list! How He works and addresses your needs may be beyond your understanding. But remember, although His ways are higher and different than our ways, He is faithful. You can depend on Him!

A Prayer for When We're Worried

Lord, You have told us not to be anxious or worried about anything,
but to present all our requests before You.
Thank You for the incredible invitation to cast our cares and burdens
on You because You care for us
and for calling us when we're weary and burdened to come to You
so You can give us rest. We do that now, Jesus.
Here are the things we're burdened and worried about....
Just like pouring water from a pitcher, we pour out our concerns to You
and ask that You would give us Your promised peace.
Amen.

Where There Is No Doctor

And we are sure of this,

that he will listen to us

whenever we ask him for anything in line with his will.

And if we really know he is listening when we talk to him

and make our requests,

then we can be sure that he will answer us.

1 JOHN 5:14–15, TLB

Yellow fever. Cholera. Typhoid. Larry and Paula thought that the World Health Organization had eradicated those plagues decades ago. But eleven injections at a local health clinic before setting out for the mission field were ample proof that these diseases were still present in their target country—Thailand.

As a new missionary couple, the Dinkins were naive about many things, but the chance of getting sick wasn't one of them. They knew that during the first twenty years of missionary work in Thailand, before the era of antibiotics and preventive medicine, the average length of service had been less than five years. If cholera, typhoid, or dysentery didn't ravage the missionaries, smallpox or malaria leveled them. Smallpox had since been eradicated, but other diseases remained. And, sure enough, the main topic of their prayers during the first six months in Central Thailand was *health*.

The more helpless you are, the better you are fitted to pray, and the more answers to prayer you will experience.

O. HALLESBY

Strive in prayer, let faith fill your heart—so will you be strong in the Lord and in the power of His might.

ANDREW MURRAY

At one point, their four-year-old son, Andy, came down with hemorrhagic fever and was throwing up blood. Larry wrapped him in a blanket, put his limp body on the gas tank of his motorcycle, and drove to the local hospital. But the hospital couldn't even provide a bed for the child. For three days, Larry and Paula stayed in the hallway nursing and praying for Andy without even a mosquito net to protect them. Help from nurses was minimal, and relatives were expected to supply food and basic care. In answer to prayer, God graciously spared their son's life, but incidences like this made them wary of local health care. Instead, they depended on their medical book, *Where There Is No Doctor*, and prayer.

One time, Larry suffered for days with dengue fever—achy joints, red eyes, and a high temperature. When his fever soared to 104 degrees, Paula decided to act. She instructed Larry to take a shower; then she applied towels soaked in ice water to his chest and forehead as a fan blew full blast on his naked body. His teeth chattering and his body trembling, Larry wondered if the cure was worse than the fever.

On another occasion, Larry came down with acute abdominal pain. The symptoms indicated acute appendicitis. Even in the midst of the extreme pain he was suffering, the prospect of an operation at the local hospital was not appealing. Nor was a bumpy five-hour bus ride to the mission hospital. Once again Larry and Paula had to lean on the Lord of grace to remove the pain and provide relief from Larry's suffering. Paula put the manual aside, placed her hands on her husband's stomach, and together they entreated the Lord for His healing touch.

God, we do not know what is causing this pain, they prayed. It seems to be the appendix, but Lord, you know how far away we are from proper health care. We ask in the name of Jesus that you remove this pain—and the infection or source of the pain as well. Amen.

Our faith in prayer can be no passing attitude that changes with the wind or with our own feelings and circumstances; it must be a fact that God hears and answers, that His ear is ever open to the cry of His children, and that the power to do what is asked of Him is commensurate with His willingness.

E. M. BOUNDS

Shortly after Paula removed her hands from Larry's stomach, his pain completely subsided. Together, they praised God for His clear answer to prayer. Larry's extremity had been God's opportunity!

Later that day, Larry asked Paula to hand him the medical manual they had been consulting. He took a Magic Marker and wrote one word in large letters after the title *Where There Is No Doctor—PRAY!*

The Dinkins are now in their twentieth year in Thailand. Over and over they've had the opportunity to test the power of prayer, not just in medical emergencies, but in all kinds of crises. Yet they often reflect upon that pivotal time during their first term on the mission field when they witnessed the power of God to intervene in a crisis at just the right moment.

When it comes to praying together as a couple, Larry and Paula believe that they still have a long way to go. But seeing God act in response to their prayers has strengthened their marriage and faith, forged them into an effective prayer team, and enhanced their ministry.

PRAYER EXERCISE

CALLING ON GOD

Look up the following verses: John 15:7; Matthew 7:7–8; and John 16:24. What is the overall theme of these verses? Why do you think we often fail to call on God for help? What scriptural promises can you and your spouse claim, right now, to encourage you to call on God? Whatever your "extremity" is today, join hearts and hands and ask Him to intervene.

Prayer is the link that connects us with God.

It is the bridge that spans every gulf

and carries us safely over every chasm of danger or need.

A. B. SIMPSON

A Word for the Year

You do not have, because you do not ask God.

JAMES 4:2

Ron and Mary have always found it a struggle to pray together. Maybe the difficulty stems from different expectations and levels of spiritual maturity or from early in their marriage when Mary wasn't much interested in praying as a couple. Mary admits that it might even be due to stubbornness on her part. In spite of that, they are both eager and obedient in praying individually for each other, and both have experienced the blessings of prayer in their own lives and in the life of their family.

Sometimes, however, the needs and the number of requests seem overwhelming. They know that the Lord has instructed them to bear each other's burdens, to petition Him for the growth of Christlike character in each other, and to bring to God every request that might be important to the other. Yet, where were they to start? And more importantly, where were they to stop?

Over the years, Ron and Mary have become convinced of the truth of James 4:2: "You do not have, because you do not ask God." They are also convinced that God wants them to ask specifically and measurably—in part so that they will notice His grace in their lives and witness His answers to their requests.

So they have devised a couple of ways to help them pray on the other person's behalf.

First, at the beginning of each January, instead of making New Year's resolutions, they each choose a word or phrase that will be their catchword throughout the year. Mary's word for 1999 was *posture*. It reflected her desire to address several areas of her life: physically, she wanted to remember to stand up straight; spiritually, she wanted to be continually in a posture of humility before the Lord; socially, she wanted to assume the posture of servanthood, putting others ahead of herself.

Intercessory prayer is part of the sovereign purpose of God. If there were no saints praying for us, our lives would be infinitely balder than they are. Consequently the responsibility of those who never intercede and who are withholding blessing from other lives is truly appalling.

OSWALD CHAMBERS

As the year went on, Mary wondered what her husband's word was. But Ron kept it a secret from her, hoping that she would be able to figure it out from his actions. Although she pestered him about it several times, Mary didn't have a clue.

On New Year's Day, as the couple was cleaning up the breakfast dishes after watching the Parade of Roses on TV, they discussed their words for the year 2000. Ron chose the words *living large* because he wanted to make the most of every moment. Mary selected the word *aware* because she wanted to be alert to God's work and presence all around her.

Then Ron told Mary what his word had been for 1999: *Mary.* In retrospect, Mary could see how Ron had made an extra effort to be with her, to court and date her, and to do thoughtful things that would make her feel cherished. She just hadn't been aware of it, poor guy! They laughed together at the appropriateness of Mary's word for the year 2000.

Another way that Ron and Mary make prayer for each other less overwhelming and more measurable is for each of them to choose three subjects that they want the other to pray for—things that need changing, areas that need growth, and decisions that need to be made.

They update the three-point list whenever they want to. Right now, Ron is praying that Mary's prayer life will become richer and more fruitful, that she will figure out how to have more energy and restful sleep, and that she'll learn to live by a schedule. Mary is praying that Ron will be less distracted so that he can focus on his projects, that he will finish things he has started, and that his prayer life will grow in richness. Likewise, they are praying for three important areas that they've chosen for each of their kids.

As Ron and Mary pray for each other, they are encouraged by tangible

Let us record our prayers on paper and mark well the answers, for many understand that the blessings they have are the answers to their own prayers!

CAMERON V. THOMPSON

We must recognize that prayer alone, prayer together, prayer for ourselves, prayer for each other, continual prayer is an essential portion of our work.

EDITH SCHAEFFER

progress. "Ron has seen a measurable improvement in his ability—and motivation—to stay 'on task,'" Mary says. "That's a big success for him." And Mary is seeing measurable answers to Ron's prayers for her. "The day after we'd shared our three support areas for prayer," she says, "I ran into a friend who had recommended a particular brand of vitamins. I was so frustrated by my lack of energy and my erratic sleep patterns that I cornered her and made an appointment to meet the next day. Twenty-four hours later I was on a new regimen, and, although the jury's still out, I already see improvement in my sleep. And my energy level, though it still fluctuates, is improving."

We...do not cease to pray for you.

COLOSSIANS 1:9,

NKJV

There is nothing that makes us love a man so much as praying for him.

WILLIAM LAW

PRAYER EXERCISE
FOOTPRINTS OF GOD'S FAITHFULNESS

Ask each other to determine three major things you can intercede for throughout the coming year. It might be a need for direction, a health issue, or a desired attitude change. It could be an area of personal struggle or weakness where God's help is especially needed. Let these needs shape your petitions for each other. Then talk from time to time about how God is working in these areas and update your intercession requests as needed.

You may also find it helpful to record God's footprints of faithfulness in your marriage and family—both to build up your own confidence in God and to leave a record behind for your children. Be assured—when you pray, you will bring blessings to your mate's life!

The Mortar in a Marriage

By wisdom a house is built,

and through understanding it is established.

PROVERBS 24:3

On a warm October afternoon, Ken and Deb walked from their townhouse down the alley toward the bank. They longed for a new home, and they were sure that the loan they were about to receive to purchase a country lot was their ticket to joy. As they strolled along, Deb envisioned her son laughing as he rode his bike up a sweeping driveway toward a large brick house with immense white pillars.

How different life will be! she thought. *No cramped fourteen-foot-wide row house on a busy city artery. No more noisy traffic. No more hearing our neighbors' arguments through the thin walls. No more roaches crawling through for a visit.*

When they pushed open the glass doors of the bank, it was as though they were walking through the doorway to a better life. The bank manager took them through the formalities, and then all that remained was for them to sign their names on the appropriate lines.

"And this payment includes our current house mortgage, right?" Ken asked.

"No," the manager corrected him. "This payment is *in addition* to whatever payments you make on your present home."

"In addition? Wait a minute…I thought…" Ken stammered. He had done all the application work; they had made the down payment for the land. How could he have been mistaken about the monthly payments?

"How can we lower the payments?" Ken asked, the feeling of panic rising in his chest.

"There's nothing I can do now—unless you want to pay a penalty and lose your down payment."

They did not want to lose their hard-earned money—or the lot. So although the two payments together far exceeded their monthly earnings, Ken and Deb reluctantly signed.

Trudging home, their feet felt chained to hundred-pound weights. A biting north wind had come up, and it raked across their faces. Even though they prayed about things regularly, Ken had been so sure that this was a good deal—and that the builder he worked for would build them an inexpensive home—that they hadn't truly sought God's guidance about it. Deb hadn't known all the details, but she had trusted Ken's judgment. Now it was apparent that he had made a grievous error.

"Where will we get another three hundred dollars each month?

If you are pressed hard by problems right now, if you are longing for changes in yourself, your marriage, and your life, you can count on this: God is in control of everything; God is involved in your problems; God has the answers and provision you need; and God has promised to provide them for you if you are willing to receive them.

ED WHEAT

How will we pay the heating bills?" Deb asked.

"I don't know, but don't worry. God will get us out of this. Just don't buy anything for a couple of months," Ken answered, trying to reassure her.

But then Ken lost his job with the builder. And then the development committee rejected the house plans they submitted. Finally, Deb became pregnant and required an emergency cesarean section to deliver their baby. Although they were thankful for the arrival of a healthy girl, the hospital bills wiped out what was left of their savings.

The best answers to prayer may be the vision and strength to meet a circumstance or assume a responsibility.

C. R. FINDLEY

Now it wasn't simply "don't buy anything for a few months"—they were stuck in a seemingly endless routine of "scrimp and do without."

As months of leanness stretched into a year, and then two, Deb struggled with resentment. *Why do I have to suffer when I've done nothing wrong? I can't bear to live like this. How could Ken have been so stupid? Help, God!*

Successful marriage is always a triangle: a man, a woman, and God.

CECIL MYERS

Despite several arguments when their feelings surfaced, Deb and Ken's nightly prayer time held their hearts together. As they sat next to each other holding hands and praying for each other and their differences and mistakes, their grudges and unforgivingness melted away.

Gradually Deb's anger dissipated, and she felt a renewed belief that God would somehow turn their nightmare into a joyful experience.

Instead of shining the harsh light of interrogation on her husband, she began to view Ken through the soft eyes of sympathy. Together, Ken and Deb began to lean on God's wisdom instead of their own and to rely on Him to meet every need.

Prayer is the recognition that if God had not engaged himself in our problems, we would still be lost in the blackness.

MAX LUCADO

Great faith in God always expresses itself in humble acknowledgment of dependency.

W. BINGHAM HUNTER

Ken found some work with another builder, and Deb began to find ways to stretch what little money they had. She trekked to garage sales, scoured recipe books for low-cost meatless dishes, and willingly accepted gifts of used clothing. They laughed about the snow fountain that spurted through the rusting floor of their truck when Ken drove through the snowy streets in winter. Then Ken found a way to keep the snow out. He used roof pitch and screws to attach the lids of coffee cans to the underside of the truck.

One critical time, when bills had to be put in the mail but Ken's employer hadn't paid him, he ran into his boss at another construction site. Before Ken could say anything, the builder yelled from his truck, "I've got a check for you!"

God didn't rescue Ken and Deb from their situation or make their problems go away, but He did make a way for them to go *through* it. Sometimes it was in the eleventh hour, but He always provided. The couple learned to work together instead of against each other, to be resourceful, to save, and to use the things they had.

They also learned to be a team. Instead of the economic hardship tearing them apart, their trials gradually drew them closer. Prayer was the mortar of their marriage, and God became the steel support behind the bricks of their lives.

After four years, they paid off the loan for the lot and began construction on their new home. Today, Ken, Deb, and their two children live in a modest brick home on the lot they purchased. There are no sweeping driveways or huge white pillars, but Ken and Deb are very grateful to live in their own home. As they look back, some of their funniest and fondest memories are of how Ken patched his truck and how thrilled Deb was to find Christmas toys for their kids still in the boxes at garage sales.

As for future decisions, the couple now holds to a firmly established principle: Get all the facts, pray for God's wisdom and guidance, and work with—not against—each other.

PRAYER EXERCISE

KEEPING SHORT ACCOUNTS

Are you living with the consequences of mistakes one of you made? Has resentment built walls between the two of you because of those mistakes? If so, come together to the throne of grace and ask for God's forgiveness to flow between you. Ask Him to help you work together as a team. Keep short accounts by forgiving each other daily. And above all, rely on God and His wisdom for the decisions you make and the trials you encounter in your lives together.

A Prayer for Provision

Jehovah-Jireh, the Lord our Provider, we praise You that You have given us
in Christ Jesus everything we need for life and godliness.
Help us to believe and have confidence in Your goodness,
Your provision, and Your promises.
While we're dealing with financial challenges,
remind us of specific times in the past when You have faithfully provided,
so our hearts will overflow with thanksgiving
instead of grumbling and complaining.
Here is our need, Lord.
We ask You to provide and fill this need in Your way and timing.
Give us wisdom in managing the financial resources You have provided.
And forgive us for leaning on our own understanding
and doing things our way instead of Your way,
for being self-sufficient instead of depending on You,
and for focusing on earthly things more than Your kingdom.
Help us to trust in You with all our heart!
Amen.

Trust for the Journey

Listen to this wise advice; follow it closely,

for it will do you good,

and you can pass it on to others:

Trust in the Lord.

P R O V E R B S   2 2 : 1 7 – 1 9 ,   T L B

ike Yorkey worked at Focus on the Family for eleven years. Not only did he love his work, but when the Focus on the Family ministry was located in Southern California, he and his family lived only two hours from his parents. Mike's only brother had died of cancer in 1988, so being near their remaining child and only grandchildren was a huge blessing to his parents.

Even so, when the organization moved from California to Colorado Springs, Mike, his wife, Nicole, son, Patrick, and daughter, Andrea, pulled up stakes and moved with the ministry. As Focus on the Family grew, so did Mike's responsibilities. He found that being part of a monthly magazine ministering in two million homes was an incredible opportunity. God also blessed his family in their new location. Mike's parents, however, were heartbroken that they were now so far away.

Then in 1997—out of the blue—Mike received a job offer from a company starting up in San Diego. Their aim was to publish a magazine that would share Christian principles with families in the corporate workplace. As Mike and Nicole prayed about the new opportunity, they said, *Lord, we're happy here, but we're asking—is this from You? Do You want us to move?*

After persistently seeking the Lord's direction for two months, Mike and Nicole were sure that God was giving them the green light to move to San Diego. Although they knew that it was risky to leave a solid ministry for a smaller organization with only four employees (Focus On the Family had more than 1300 employees, and Mike had never missed a paycheck), they felt that it was God's will for them to go. So with great hopes, they moved to San Diego.

The Yorkeys found a home to lease and a wonderful Christian school for their children. And they were thrilled to be close to Mike's parents again. The kids adjusted well in school and began to grow in their personal walks with Christ.

But before the end of the first year, Mike was asked *not* to cash his paychecks due to cash-flow problems. Just a temporary glitch, he was told—the company's financial problems would soon be resolved. In the meantime, the Yorkeys' lease was almost up. They had made an offer to purchase a house, and the time for closing was drawing closer.

The power of God is put at the disposal of praying souls; and upon the earth wonderful changes...take place. Prayer has gone up to heaven, found acceptance, and returned in answers of almighty power, as moisture goes up in vapor and returns in rain.

A. T. Pierson

Mike kept working diligently, but suddenly his paychecks stopped altogether. From January to June he worked every day, trying to keep the company going. During that time he did not receive a paycheck. As they neared the end of their resources, the Yorkeys faced enormous financial uncertainties. They didn't know how they were going to pay for everything—housing, utilities, groceries, clothing for the kids, tuition for the next year of school, and taxes.

Mike and Nicole went to their knees in prayer and laid everything out before the Lord—their needs, Mike's career, the kids' schooling. *Should we move to a cheaper part of the country?* they asked. *Should we go back to Colorado Springs? Do we stay here and take the kids out of school? Lord, we really believe that You directed us here to be near Mike's parents, yet the cost has drained us. We're trusting and depending on You.*

Things got tighter, and one day Mike and Nicole felt very anxious. But God took them back to Proverbs 22:17–19, which encouraged them to listen to God and take to heart His wise advice. *Trust* was God's single word to them. They had heeded His direction by moving back to Southern California. Now He was reminding them to *trust* instead of panic. *Trust in the Lord!* That is what they clung to when there was nothing else.

A few days later they received a phone call from the Christian school office informing them that their tuition for the remainder of the school year had been taken care of—another couple had come in and paid the bill in full.

God's will on earth can only be secured by prayer.

E. M. BOUNDS

As we ask for His will to be made known, for His guidance for the next step, we need to ask with a determination that we will do His will…whatever it is.

EDITH SCHAEFFER

Mike and Nicole hit the floor on their knees. *Wow, You're unbeliev-able, Lord!* From the depth of their hearts they thanked and praised God for how He had provided. There were still other challenges to face, but they had received a remarkable demonstration that they weren't alone—God was with them, and He could be *trusted*.

With the tuition paid, the Yorkeys were able to squeeze by. Mike began writing full time and received several contracts for book-length projects. Gradually things began to turn around. There have been tight moments since, but when stress comes, Mike and Nicole remember God's provision for their journey and His encouragement to pray, hang on, and trust Him.

The value of persistent prayer is not that he will hear us...but that we will finally hear him.

WILLIAM McGILL

PRAYER EXERCISE

PERSEVERING—THE KEY TO ANSWERED PRAYER

The classic little book *Practice of Prayer* offers this helpful passage: "People often ask 'How long should I pray? Shouldn't I finally come to the place where I stop praying and leave the matter in God's hands?' The only answer is this: *Pray until what you pray for has been accomplished or until you have complete assurance in your heart that it will be.*"[7]

Review the Bible stories of those who persisted in prayer: the man who wouldn't give up at midnight (Luke 11:5–8); the blind man who wouldn't stop crying out to the Lord (Mark 10:46–52); and the widow who wore out a judge with her pleading (Luke 18:1–8). In each case, what was the outcome?

Whatever immovable or insurmountable situation you're facing, persevere in prayer. You will grow in the God-given assurance that He is always with you. Perseverance is the key to answered prayer and untold blessings in your life!

A Last Word to Couples

Someone once said, "It is the heart that prays; it is to the voice of the heart that God listens; and it is the heart that He answers." Maybe that is precisely why we sometimes avoid prayer with our spouse—it's just so heart-to-heart.

But, as you have seen through the stories in this book, the heart-to-heart nature of prayer is part of the beauty of praying together as a couple. When you hear each other's "voice of the heart"—the feelings and longings underneath the surface—your hearts are knit together in new ways. Coldness and indifference can melt away in a few tender moments together. Who knows what might come from experiencing God's presence in prayer? You could find emotional healing, a new sense of unity, a physical relationship sparked anew when the embers were dying, or a special blessing in the lives of your children.

Every time you pray together, you are letting God into your lives and into the particular situation you talk to Him about. In those moments of prayer as a couple, God wraps His arms around each of you and bridges any gaps between you. No matter how difficult the situation, there is no substitute for the flood of peace that results from a husband and wife praying together. There is no situation so dark or problem so hopeless that God can't shine His light and provide help. And most importantly, when you pray faithfully through a crisis or extremely painful situation, you'll find that the difficulty actually brings you closer together instead of tearing you apart.

As you have read the stories in this book, you have seen the power of praying couples demonstrated over and over again. Hopefully, you and your spouse have also talked about your prayer life—perhaps how your styles are different or in what ways you need to be flexible and accept each other so that you can harmonize in prayer.

So now let me encourage you to pray! As you do, the watching world will see in your marriage a living picture of the intimate relationship between Jesus and His bride, the church.

May God bless your marriage, shine His face upon your life together, pour out His Spirit and joy on your family, and give you His peace.

About the Author

Cheri Fuller is a dynamic inspirational speaker and author of twenty-six other books. She won the Gold Medallion Award in 1998, and her *When Families Pray* was a 2000 Gold Medallion finalist. Her bestselling *When Mothers Pray* is giving moms throughout the U. S. and the world hope and inspiration to pray for their children.

Cheri is a contributing editor for *Today's Christian Woman* and serves on the editorial board of *Pray!* magazine. Her articles have appeared in *Focus on the Family, Family Circle, ParentLife,* and other periodicals, and she has been a guest on hundreds of radio and TV programs, including *Focus on the Family,* Moody's *Mid-day Connection,* and *At Home—Live!* She is also the leader of a local Moms In Touch group.

Cheri's ministry, Families Pray USA!, encourages parents and teachers to raise up a dynamic young generation of prayer warriors and to pray together for our country, our communities, and our families.

Cheri and her husband, Holmes, have three grown children and three grandchildren. She loves encouraging others as she speaks at women's retreats and conferences. Her Web site, www.CheriFuller.com, features her biweekly columns "Mothering By Heart" and "Families Pray USA!" For information on speaking engagements, contact her at cheri@cherifuller.com or P.O. Box 770493, Oklahoma City, OK 73177.

1. Commissioned Research entitled "Evangelical Christians," Gallup Research Corporation Summary Report, May 1991; Jack D. Jernigan and Steven L. Nock, "Religiosity and Family Stability: Do Families That Pray Together Stay Together?" Department of Sociology, University of Virginia, November 1983.

2. "Roses" story, adapted from Pam and Bill Farrell, *Pure Pleasure* (Colorado Springs, Colo.: InterVarsity Press, 1994).

3. Charlie Shedd, "The MP Interview," in *Marriage Partnership,* Fall 1992, 46–7.

4. Adapted from Dave and Claudia Arp, *Quiet Whispers from God's Heart for Couples* (Nashville, Tenn.: J. Countryman/Thomas Nelson, 1999). Also see the Arps' marriage website at: www.marriagealive.com.

5. Lin's Web site is www.childrensprayernet.org.

6. In His Name Ministries, Inc., Web site www.inhisname.org, e-mail dee@inhisname.org

7. *Streams in the Desert,* ed. L. B. Cowman (Grand Rapids, Mich.: Zondervan Publishing House, 1997), 184–5.

PRAYER *by*
Cheri Fuller

When Mothers Pray

This bestselling source of teaching, stories, and hope
will inspire and revitalize readers as they learn what
happens *When Mothers Pray.*
ISBN I-57673-935-X

When Families Pray

Designed for the entire family, this book of
devotions, stories, and activities will guide children
and adults into a meaningful prayer life that will
reap visible rewards for life.
ISBN I-57673-888-4

When Children Pray

A godsend for busy parents who recognize the importance of teaching children
to pray, but aren't confident they know how. It also affirms the incredible power
of childrens' prayers with true stories of how God answered them.
ISBN I-57673-894-9

www.whenwepray.com

whenwepray.com

God answers prayer everyday. This Web site is dedicated to sharing how ordinary people: families, kids, couples, and communities are remarkably and supernaturally touched by a loving God.

- Read answered prayers by topic

- Submit your own answered prayer

- Encourage a friend or family member by emailing them one of these encouraging stories of answered prayer.

- Gain insights and valuable resources on praying with your children, spouse, and family.

Stop by whenwepray.com *and be encouraged and inspired by the God who is always listening.*